Praise for *The Imitation of Christ*

The Imitation of Christ is one of the great spiritual works of the Church. More than five hundred years later, it remains not just a classic, but a road map to the life the Lord wants each of us to live.

—Timothy Michael Cardinal Dolan
Archbishop of New York

This influential book is an incredible gift to this century. James Watkins has stayed true to the original text but in language that continues to speak from the soul of Thomas à Kempis to the soul of a twenty-first-century seeker. A message for which our world has deep hunger. This is literally a soul-changing, ultimately world-changing book; a must for every person serious about being a Christ-follower.

—Jo Anne Lyon, Founder of World Hope International,
General Superintendent, The Wesleyan Church,
Member, President's Advisory Council on
Faith-Based and Neighborhood Partnerships

Thomas à Kempis's *The Imitation of Christ* is a timeless classic. Watkins has succeeded in providing a clear and accurate rendering of this great volume for a new generation of Catholic and Protestants alike. I'm looking forward to reading this many times.

—Rev. Randolph Sly, Priest and
Personal Ordinariate of the Chair of St. Peter

The Imitation of Christ devotional is truly a gift to the church. Watkins provides timeless, profound truths in everyday language, introducing modern Christians to the power of Thomas à Kempis's words and life's work. A deeply moving, wholly convicting, and truly life-altering book.

—Mary DeMuth, Author of *Worth Living: How God's Wild Love for You Changes Everything*

Each morning I eagerly go to this modern version of *The Imitation of Christ* knowing it will convict and teach my spirit, giving me spiritual focus throughout the day. It is the best devotional I've found in many years.

—Lissa Halls Johnson, Author and Speaker

THE IMITATION OF
CHRIST

THE IMITATION OF
CHRIST

CLASSIC DEVOTIONS IN TODAY'S LANGUAGE

THOMAS À KEMPIS

COMPILED AND EDITED BY JAMES N. WATKINS

WORTHY℠
Inspired

Published by Worthy Inspired, an imprint of Worthy Publishing Group, a division of Worthy Media, Inc., One Franklin Park, 6100 Tower Circle, Suite 210, Franklin, TN 37067.

WORTHY is a registered trademark of Worthy Media, Inc.

HELPING PEOPLE EXPERIENCE THE HEART OF GOD

Library of Congress Cataloging-in-Publication Data

Imitatio Christi. English.
  The imitation of Christ : classic devotions in today's language / Thomas à Kempis ; compiled and edited by James N. Watkins.
    pages cm
  ISBN 978-1-61795-676-8 (hardcover)
  1. Devotional literature. 2. Meditations—Early works to 1800. 3. Spiritual life—Catholic Church—Early works to 1800. 4. Catholic Church—Doctrines—Early works to 1800. I. Thomas à Kempis, 1380-1471. II. Watkins, James, 1952—editor. III. Title.
  BV4821.W38 2015
  242--dc23

2015031887

All Scripture quotations, unless otherwise indicated, are taken from the *Holy Bible, New Living Translation,* copyright ©1996, 2004, 2007, 2013 by Tyndale House Foundation. Used by permission of Tyndale House Publishers, Inc., Carol Stream, Illinois 60188. All rights reserved.

ISBN: 978-1-61795-676-8

For foreign and subsidiary rights, contact rights@worthypublishing.com

Cover design: Faceout Studio, Jeff Miller
Cover Illustration: Getty Images

Printed in the United States of America

15 16 17 18 19 20 21 RRD 10 9 8 7 6 5 4 3 2 1

DEDICATION

Dedicated to the original author, Thomas à Kempis,
whose writing of *The Imitation of Christ*
dramatically and forever changed my life.

And, of course, to the One whom I am trying to imitate.

CONTENTS

Teachable

Wise

Trusting

Obedient

Self-Sacrificing

Humble

INTRODUCTION

"The one who follows me will not walk in darkness,"
says the Lord. These words of Christ teach us
how far we must imitate his life and character,
if we seek true understanding and deliverance
for deception of our hearts and minds.
Let us, then, most earnestly study and dwell upon
the life of Jesus Christ. Christ's teachings surpass
all the teachings of holy men, and if we have
his Spirit we find spiritual nourishment.

Thomas à Kempis

Thomas à Kempis's *The Imitation of Christ* changed my life. I was hustling to become a rich and famous author/speaker when I was confronted by this convicting book's message: "Be content to be unknown and not respected." But I could serve Christ much more effectively as a *New York Times* best-selling author and globe-trotting speaker! I quickly discovered that while I had a degree in theology, and had been writing Christian books and articles most of my professional life, à Kempis taught a close, deep relationship with

Jesus Christ that I didn't possess! I knew Christ, but I didn't *know* Christ. I have read through *The Imitation of Christ* at least ten times now, and each time, I find myself knowing Christ in closer and deeper ways. I'm learning that he must increase and I must decrease—especially on book covers.

So, I invite you to join millions of readers who, over the past five hundred years, have become more like Christ through this amazing book.

The devotional classic, second only to the Bible in sales, was written anonymously in Latin in the Netherlands. Thomas Haemmerlein (1380–1471), better known as Thomas à Kempis, is generally credited as the author/editor, but purposely avoided claiming its authorship. He wrote, "Do not let the writer's authority or learning—be it little or great—influence you, but let the love of pure truth attract you to read. Do not ask, 'Who said this?' but pay attention to what is said." In fact, much of the writing is borrowed from the Bible, the early Church fathers, and medieval monks.

He spent seventy-two years as a member of the Brothers of the Common Life at the Mount St. Agnes Monastery in Deventer, Holland, serving as a "canon regular." Unlike a monk, who limited his ministry within the walls of a monastery, this title describes a religious cleric who lived in the community, but served in local congregations. He spent his time writing biographies of members of his order as well as copying the Bible by hand at least four times. He also was in charge of instructing young members of his order. In that capacity, he wrote four devotional booklets, which later were combined into *The Imitation of Christ*. At times, he wrote as the disciple and at other times as if Christ were speaking directly to the student.

The hand-copied manuscripts of the book were first circulated as early as 1420, with its first publication in English in 1696.

Through the centuries, the book has been recommended by such diverse leaders as John Wesley, the founder of Methodism, and Thomas Merton, the popular twentieth-century author and Catholic monk. The Jesuits, a Catholic order of priests and brothers, honored the book. Their founder, St. Ignatius of Loyola, was inspired by *The Imitation of Christ* to formulate his own *Spiritual Exercises*. The book has been published as more than six thousand editions in more than fifty languages.

Because *The Imitation of Christ* has had a most profound effect on my spiritual life, I am pleased to offer this updated version arranged for devotional reading. I have carefully updated William Benham's 1874 translation with modern and inclusive language that remains faithful to the original message. Catholic scholar Michael Fraley compared my modernization with the original Latin text and made valuable suggestions to assure accuracy. For clarity, I have added headings to indicate who is speaking, as well as biblical passages which introduce and reinforce the theme of each chapter. Passages taken directly from Scripture have also been attributed.

I pray this edition of the classic work will provide a new generation of readers the life-changing message of *The Imitation of Christ*.

PART I

IMITATING CHRIST

1

ON THE IMITATION
OF CHRIST

Imitate God, therefore, in everything you do,
because you are his dear children. Live a life
filled with love, following the example of Christ.

Ephesians 5:1–2

The Disciple

These are the words of Christ: "If you follow me, you won't
have to walk in darkness" (John 8:12). They teach us how
thoroughly we must imitate his life and character if we
desire true understanding and freedom from our own
deceptive hearts and minds. And so, may we earnestly study
and meditate on the life of Jesus Christ.

Christ's teachings surpass all of the great holy writers
of the past. If we have his Spirit, we find spiritual nourishment. Unfortunately there are many people who frequently
hear the words of Christ but have little desire to follow
them and so do not have the mind of Christ.

What does it profit us to engage in deep discussions about the Father, Son, and Holy Spirit if we lack humility and are displeasing to God? Truly, deep and profound words do not make a person holy and upright, but a good life is what makes us dear to God. I would rather experience sorrow for my ungodly thoughts and actions than simply be skillful in defining "repentance." If we know the whole Bible and the teachings of all the philosophers, what does all this benefit us without the love and grace of God? It is completely futile unless we love God and serve only him. This is the highest wisdom: to put earthly values behind us and to reach forward to the heavenly kingdom.

It is futile to strive for earthly things and to trust in riches that will perish. It is futile to desire honors and lift up ourselves. It is futile to be ruled by the desires of our physical body, for this will only bring misery in the end. It is futile to desire a long life and to care little for a good life. It is futile to concentrate on the here and now and not look forward to the things which are eternal. It is futile to love temporary things and not strive toward eternal joy.

Always keep this saying in mind: "The eye is not satisfied with visible things. Neither is the ear content with hearing." And so, let us strive to turn our hearts from the love of things that are visible and concentrate on the things that are invisible. If we are controlled by our own physical desires, we will corrupt our conscience and destroy the grace of God.

Book 1 Chapter 1

2

ON CHRIST AS THE WAY, THE TRUTH, THE LIFE

"I am the way, the truth, and the life.
No one can come to the Father except through me."

John 14:6

The Christ

My friend, the more you let go of your own desires, the more you will become like me. When you have no desire for outward things, only then you will enjoy internal peace. When you stop living for yourself, you will grow into union with me. I want you to learn perfect self-denial and to live as I desire without disagreeing or complaining. "I am the way, the truth, and the life. No one can come to the Father except through me" (John 14:6). Without my way you cannot go. Without my truth you cannot know. And without my life you cannot grow. I am the way which you must follow, the truth you must believe, and the life for which you must hope. I am the way never changing, the truth never failing, and the life never ending. I am the straight way, the supreme truth and the true, blessed, and uncreated life. "And you will know the truth, and the truth will set you free" (John 8:32). Only then will you enjoy eternal life.

"If you want to receive eternal life, keep the commandments" (Matthew 19:17). If you want to know the truth, believe in me. If you want to be perfect, sell all that you have. If you want to be my disciple, deny yourself. If you want to possess the blessed life, give up the life you now have. If you want to be exalted in heaven, humble yourself in this world. If you want to reign with me, bear the cross with me, for only the servants of the cross find the blessed life and true light.

The Disciple

O Lord Jesus, for as much as your life was righteous and despised by the world, may I imitate you in despising the world, for "students are not greater than their teacher, and slaves are not greater than their master" (Matthew 10:24). Let your servant model your life, because in it is salvation and true holiness. Anything I read or hear besides it does not refresh me or give me delight.

The Christ

"Those who accept my commandments and obey them are the ones who love me. And because they love me, my Father will love them. And I will love them and reveal myself to each of them" (John 14:21). They will sit down with me in my Father's kingdom.

The Disciple

O Lord Jesus, as you have said and promised, please let it be so. And help me to prove myself worthy. I have received the cross from your hands. I have carried it, even as you have laid it upon me, and I will continue to carry it until I die. Truly the life of a devoted servant is the cross, but it leads to paradise. I have begun the journey of the cross. May I not turn back nor leave it.

Come, my brothers and sisters, let us go forward together. Jesus will be with us. For Jesus' sake, we have taken up this cross. For Jesus' sake, let us persevere as we carry it. He is our leader and example. He will help us carry it. Look! Our king enters in before us, and he will fight for us. Let us follow bravely, fearing no terror. Let us be prepared to die bravely in battle. Let us not be dishonored by fleeing from the cross.

Book 3 Chapter 56

3

ON OFFERING ALL OF
OURSELVES TO GOD

---

*And so, dear brothers and sisters, I plead with you
to give your bodies to God because of all he has
done for you. Let them be a living and holy sacrifice—
the kind he will find acceptable. This is truly the way
to worship him. Don't copy the behavior and customs
of this world, but let God transform you into
a new person by changing the way you think.
Then you will learn to know God's will for you,
which is good and pleasing and perfect.*

Romans 12:1-2

The Disciple

"Everything in the heavens and on earth is yours, O LORD"
(1 Chronicles 29:11). I desire to offer myself up to you
as a freewill offering: continually yours forever. "I have
watched your people offer their gifts willingly and joyously"
(1 Chronicles 29:17). So I offer myself to you today to be

your servant forever—in humble submission and with the sacrifice of perpetual praise.

Lord, I lay before you all the sins and offences that I have committed from the day when I was first able to sin until this hour. Please consume and burn every sin with the fire of your love and mercy. And may you cleanse all the stains of my sins and purify my conscience from all guilt. Restore me to your favor, which by sinning I have lost. Fully forgive all my sins and mercifully grant to me your peace.

What can I do concerning my sins except humbly confess them, regret them, and unceasingly plead for your pardon? I ask for your grace so you may hear me when I stand before you, O my God. All my sins displease and grieve me. I will regret them as long as I live. I earnestly desire to repent truly and to make restitution as far as I can. Forgive me, O God. Forgive my sins for your holy name's sake. Save my soul, which you have redeemed with your precious blood. See, I commit myself to your mercy, I resign myself to your hands. Deal with me—not according to my selfishness and sinfulness—but according to your loving-kindness.

I also offer to you all my goodness, though it is so little and imperfect. Please mend and purify me, making me pleasing and acceptable in your sight. May I constantly be drawn toward your holy perfection. In addition, please bring this lazy and useless creature that I am to a happy and blessed end.

I ask you, with all the sincerity, to provide for every need of my parents, friends, brothers, sisters, and all who are dear to me and that you love. May they sense they are being assisted by your grace, enriched by your comfort, protected from dangers, freed from pains, and delivered from all evils. May they joyfully give you abundant thanks.

I also pray for those who have injured me for no reason, have made me sad, have spoken evil against me, or have caused me any loss or displeasure. And please pardon me for all the times I have knowingly or ignorantly made others sad, disturbed, burdened, and scandalized by *my* words or deeds. Take away, O Lord, from our hearts all suspicion, resentment, anger, conflicts, and whatever harms and diminishes love between all people. Have mercy, Lord, on those who beg for your mercy. Give grace to the needy. And make us worthy to enjoy your grace and go forward to life eternal. Amen.

Book 4 Chapter 9

4

ON TAKING UP
CHRIST'S CROSS

---

*Then Jesus said to his disciples, "If any of you wants
to be my follower, you must turn from your selfish ways,
take up your cross, and follow me."*

Matthew 16:24

The Disciple

Jesus has many lovers of his heavenly kingdom but few
bearers of his cross. He has many seekers of comfort but few
willing to face troubles and trial. He finds many companions at his table but few with him in fasting. Many desire to
rejoice with him, but few are willing to undergo adversity
for his sake. Many follow Jesus that they may eat of his
bread, but few are willing to drink of the cup of his passion.
Many are astonished at his miracles, but few follow after the
shame of his cross. Many love Jesus so long as no troubles
happen to them. Many praise him and bless him, so long as
they receive comforts from him. But if Jesus hides himself

and seems to withdraw from them for even a little while, they immediately begin complaining or feel a great sense of dejection.

But those who love Jesus for Jesus' sake—and not for the comforts he gives to them—praise him in all suffering and sorrow just as they do in the greatest blessings. And if he should never give them another blessing, they would nevertheless continue to always praise him and give him thanks.

Oh, how powerful is the pure love of Jesus—unmixed with any material benefits or love of self! Shouldn't all those constantly seeking his blessing be called mercenaries? Don't those who are always seeking their own gain and advantage show themselves to be lovers of themselves more than lovers of Christ? Who can be found who is willing to serve God altogether for no earthly benefit?

Rarely is anyone so spiritual as to be free from all selfish thoughts? Who can find a person truly poor in spirit and free from the love of created things? People may give away all their goods, yet that is nothing. They may do many good deeds to attempt restitution for their evil deeds, but that is still a small thing. And though one may understand all knowledge, that is still far from perfection. And even if we have great virtue and zealous devotion, there is still much lacking in each of us.

Yes, one thing is the most necessary. What is it then? To give up all things, to reject all self-love, and to completely do all that we know to be required of God himself. Let us who serve Christ not feel highly esteemed, but know what the Truth has pronounced: "In the same way, when you obey me you should say, 'We are unworthy servants who have simply done our duty'" (Luke 17:10). Then we will know we are truly poor, naked in spirit, and able to say with the psalmist, "Turn to me and have mercy, for I am alone and in deep distress" (Psalm 25:16). Nevertheless, no people are richer, stronger, freer than those who know how to give unselfishly and be lowly in their own eyes.

Book 2 Chapter 11

5

ON THE ROYAL WAY
OF THE CROSS

*The message of the cross is foolish to those who are
headed for destruction! But we who are
being saved know it is the very power of God.*

1 Corinthians 1:18

The Disciple

This seems a hard saying to many: "If any of you wants to
be my follower, you must turn from your selfish ways, take
up your cross, and follow me" (Matthew 16:24). But do
not fear, for the cross leads to heaven. In the cross is health,
in the cross is life, in the cross is protection from enemies,
in the cross is heavenly delight, in the cross is strength of
mind, in the cross is joy of the spirit, in the cross is the
height of good deeds, in the cross is holy living. There is
no health of the soul nor hope of eternal life except in
the cross.

So, we must take up our cross and follow Jesus. Only then, will we enter into eternal life. He went before us bearing his cross and died for us on the cross, so that we would bear our crosses. So, if we die to ourselves for him, we will also live with him. And if we participate in his sufferings, we will also participate in his glory.

Everything depends on the cross, and everything is conditioned on dying. There is no other way to life, truth, and inward peace except in the way of the cross and of daily self-sacrifice. Then, no matter what we seek or desire, we will find it. We will find no higher way above nor safer way below than the way of the holy cross. So, whether we suffer willingly or unwillingly, we take up the cross.

Sometimes we will feel forsaken by God. Sometimes we will be annoyed with our neighbor, or more often be frustrated and impatient with ourselves. Still, we cannot be delivered nor eased by any remedy or comfort. We must bear the cross for as long as God determines. He will allow us to suffer troubles without comfort, so we must submit ourselves fully to it, for by trials and troubles we will be made more humble. People do not understand in their own hearts the suffering of Christ so well as the ones who are suffering themselves. The cross, therefore, is always ready and waiting for us. We cannot flee from it. If we turn above, below, outward, or inward, we will still find the cross. We must yield patiently to it if we are to have internal peace and gain the everlasting crown.

If we willingly bear the cross, it will bear us. If we bear it unwillingly, we will greatly increase the weight and make it a burden for ourselves. We must bear it. And if we refuse one cross, there is no doubt we will encounter another cross—far heavier.

Don't think we can escape what no mortal has been able to avoid. Which of the saints in the world has lived without the cross and troubles and trial? Not even Jesus Christ, our Lord, lived one hour of his life without the anguish of his cross. "And [Jesus] said, 'Yes, it was written long ago that the Messiah would suffer and die and rise from the dead on the third day'" (Luke 24:46).

The whole life of Christ was a cross and martyrdom, so why do we chase after relaxation and joyous living? If we desire to avoid suffering, we are wrong, for this whole mortal life is full of miseries and circled with crosses. And the higher people advance in the spirit, the heavier the crosses they will often find. The sorrow of feeling Christ's banishment increases with the strength of his love.

But people who are afflicted like this are not without refreshment or comfort, because as they bear Christ's cross they feel themselves becoming more Christ-like. For while they willingly submitted themselves to it, every burden of troubles and trial is turned into an assurance of divine comfort. The more their bodies are tested with pain, the more their spirit is strengthened mightily by inward grace. Often, they are so greatly comforted that they begin to desire troubles and adversity. Because of the love they feel in suffering the cross as Christ did, they would not choose to be free from sorrow and troubles. This is not the natural reaction of humans! This is the grace of Christ. It has such power and energy in the weak flesh, that what a human would naturally hate and flee, actually draws them to the cross through the power of the Spirit.

It is not in our nature to bear the cross, to love the cross, to bring our bodies into subjection, to flee from honors, to bear criticism meekly, to discipline ourselves, to bear all adversities and losses, and to desire no prosperity in this world. If we look inside ourselves, we will find none of this. But if we trust the Lord, endurance will be given to us from heaven, and the world and our bodily desires will obey our commands. If we are armed with faith, we will not even fear our adversary, the devil. We must suffer many trials and troubles to enter into the kingdom of God.

Book 2 Chapter 12

PART II

IMITATING CHRIST'S CHARACTER

6

ON THE POWER OF
DIVINE LOVE

Then Christ will make his home in your hearts
as you trust in him, your roots will grow down
into God's love and keep you strong.
And may you have the power to understand,
as all God's people should, how wide,
how long, how high, and how deep his love is.

Ephesians 3:17-18

The Disciple

"All praise to God, the Father of our Lord Jesus Christ.
God is our merciful Father and the source of all comfort"
(2 Corinthians 1:3). I give thanks to you, Lord. You refresh
me with your own comfort—even when I am unworthy of
any comfort. I bless and glorify you continually through
your only Son and the Holy Spirit, the comforter, forever
and ever. O Lord God, holy lover of my soul, when you
come into my heart my entire being rejoices. You are my

glory and the joy of my heart. You are my hope and my refuge in the day of my trouble.

But because I am still weak in love and imperfect in virtue, I need to be strengthened and comforted by you. So, you often visit me and instruct me with your holy discipline. Deliver me from evil passions, and cleanse my heart from all unholy desires. May I be healed and thoroughly cleansed within so I may be ready to love, strong to suffer, and steadfast to endure.

Love is a great thing: a virtue above all others. Love alone makes every heavy burden light and equalizes every inequality. For it bears heavy weights and creates no burden. It makes every bitter thing sweet and good tasting. The love of Jesus inspires us to do great works and motivates with a continual desire to be more like him. Love desires to be raised up and not to be held down by any earthly thing. Love desires to be free and liberated from all earthly desires so its power may not be hindered. It is not entangled by any worldly prosperity or overcome by adversity. Nothing is sweeter than love, nothing stronger, nothing loftier, nothing broader, nothing more pleasant, nothing fuller or better in heaven or on earth than the love that was born of God. Only God can pour this love into us.

When we love, we soar, run, and are glad—free and unhindered. We give generously to all, because of what we have received from the God of love, who is high above all and from whom every good flows and moves forward. We do not seek gifts, but turn to the Giver above all good things. Love often knows no measure, but overflows above all measure. Love feels no burden, doesn't consider the effort and strives to accomplish more than it is able to do. This love doesn't plead impossibility, because it judges all things that are lawful to be possible. It is strong and therefore fulfills everything and is successful wherever it may go.

Love is watchful, and though sleeping still keeps watch; though fatigued, it is not weary; though pressured, it is not forced; and though alarmed, it is not terrified. Like a living flame and burning torch, it breaks through darkness and overcomes triumphantly. For the passionate love of the soul is a powerful sound in the ears of God saying, "My God, my beloved! You are all mine, and I am all yours."

O God, enlarge love in me, so I may learn to taste with my whole heart how sweet it is to love, to be dissolved, and to swim in love. Let me be lifted by love, elevated above myself through exceeding fervor and admiration. Let me sing the song of love, let me follow you, my Beloved on high. Let my soul exhaust itself in your praise, exulting with love. Let me love you more than myself, not loving myself except for your sake, and all those who truly love you, as the law of love commands. That love shines brightly from you.

Love is swift, sincere, pleasant, gentle, strong, patient, wise, and not self-seeking. But wherever love seeks after its own desires, it falls. Love is wise, humble, and upright; not weak, not fickle, nor longing for futile things; sober, steadfast, quiet, and guarded in all the senses. Love is submissive and obedient to all who are in authority, humble and lowly in its own sight, devout and grateful toward God, faithful and always trusting in him even when God hides his face, for without sorrow we cannot live in love.

He who is not ready to suffer all things and to conform to the will of the God of love is not worthy to be called a lover of God. Divine love urges the one who loves to embrace willingly all hard and bitter things for the beloved's sake and not to be drawn away from it because of hardship.

Book 3 Chapter 5

7

ON THE GREATNESS OF
CHRIST'S LOVE

*When we were utterly helpless, Christ came at just
the right time and died for us sinners. Now, most people
would not be willing to die for an upright person,
though someone might perhaps be willing to die for
a person who is especially good. But God showed
his great love for us by sending Christ to die
for us while we were still sinners.*

Romans 5:6-8

The Disciple

Trusting in your goodness and great mercy, O Lord, I draw
near: the sick to the Healer, the hungering and thirsting
to the Fountain of life, the poverty-stricken to the King of
heaven, the servant to the Lord, the creature to the Creator,
the desolate to my own gentle Comforter. But why do you
come to me? Who am I that you should offer me yourself?
How does a sinner dare to appear before you? And how

do you graciously come to the sinner? You know your servant, and you know that he has in himself no good thing for which you should grant him this grace. I confess therefore my own selfishness and sinfulness. I acknowledge your goodness. I praise your tenderness, and I give you thanks for your exceeding great love. For you do this for your own sake, not for my goodness, but that your goodness may be more evident to me, your charity more abundantly poured out on me, and your humility more perfectly given to me.

O sweet and tender Jesus, what reverence, what thanksgiving is due to you with perpetual praise for the receiving of your sacred body and blood. This is dignity that no one is able to express. But what should I think about as I approach my Lord? I who am unworthy; yet nevertheless I long devoutly to receive you? What would be a better and more beneficial meditation for me than utter humiliation of myself before you and praise of your infinite goodness toward me? I praise you, O my God, and exalt you for evermore. I despise myself and cast myself down before you in my sinfulness.

You are the Saint of saints, and I am the worst of sinners. Look how you stoop down to me. I am not worthy to look at you, but you come to me. You want to be with me. You invite me to your celebration of Communion. You give me the heavenly food and bread to eat: "the living bread that came down from heaven" (John 6:51) and gives life to the world.

Look how this love graciously shines upon us. What great giving of thanks and praise is due to you, Jesus, for these benefits! Oh, how praiseworthy and profitable to our spirits when you established this sacrament. How sweet and pleasant is the feast when you gave yourself for food! Oh, how admirable is your working. Lord, how mighty your power, how unspeakable your truth! For you spoke the word, and all things were made just as you commanded.

O Lord my God, very God and very man, what a wonderful thing, worthy of faith, and surpassing all the understanding of humankind, that you give yourself to us. Your bread and wine is inexhaustible food. You, O Lord of all, who have need of nothing, have desired to dwell in us. You have consecrated and instituted this mystery of Communion for both your honor and for a symbol of your death which gives us life.

Rejoice, O my soul, and give thanks to God for so great a gift and precious comfort left to us in this vale of tears. For as often as we meditate on this mystery, we celebrate the work of your redemption and are made partakers of all the merits of Christ. For the love of Christ never grows less, and the greatness of his sacrifice is never exhausted. So, by continual renewal of our spirits, let us carefully consider the great mystery of salvation. So come with new joy each time you partake of Communion. Celebrate Christ descending into the virgin's womb, becoming man, hanging on the cross, suffering, and dying for the salvation of all humankind.

Book 4 Chapter 2

8

ON THE INTIMATE LOVE
OF JESUS

---

*"I no longer call you slaves, because a master
doesn't confide in his slaves. Now you are my friends,
since I have told you everything the Father told me."*

John 15:15

The Disciple

When Jesus is present, all is well, and nothing seems hard,
But when Jesus is absent, *everything* is hard. When Jesus is
silent, we have no comfort; but if Jesus speaks a single word
to our spirit, the comfort we experience is great. Did not
Mary rise up quickly from the place where she wept when
Martha said to her, "The Teacher is here and wants to see
you" (John 11:28). Happy is the hour when Jesus calls us
from tears to the joy of the Spirit! How dry and hard we are
without Jesus! How senseless and proud if we desire anything besides or beyond Jesus! Is this not a greater loss than
if we should lose the whole world?

What can the world profit us without Jesus? To be without Jesus is the deepest, darkest hell, but to be with Jesus is the highest, sweetest paradise. If Jesus is with us, no enemy can hurt us. One who finds Jesus finds a good treasure—good above all good. But one who loses Jesus loses much—more than the whole world. The person who lives with Jesus is most rich, but the person who lives without Jesus is most poor.

It is great skill to know how to live with Jesus and great wisdom to know how to embrace him. If we are humble and peaceable, Jesus will be with us. Be godly and quiet, and he will remain with us. However, we can quickly drive Jesus away and lose his favor if we turn from him to other things. And if we have put him to flight and lost him, to whom will we flee, and whom then will we seek for a friend? Without a friend we cannot live long, and if Jesus is not our friend above all, we will be sad and desolate. It is madness, therefore, to trust or try to find joy in any other. It is preferable to have the whole world against us than Jesus offended with us. So, we must love him sincerely and supremely above all that is near and dear to us.

Let all be loved for Jesus' sake, but love him for his own. Jesus Christ alone is to be supremely loved, for he alone is good and faithful above all friends. For his sake and in him, let both enemies and friends be dear to us, and pray for them all that they may know and love him. Never desire to be praised or loved because these belong to God alone. And we must not wish that people trust us, nor give ourselves up to the love of any, but let Jesus be in us and in every good person.

We ought to be pure and free within ourselves and not entangled by any created thing. We must bring an empty and clean heart to God, if we desire to be ready to see how gracious the Lord is. And truly, unless we are drawn by his grace, we will not attain to this. Let us cast out and dismiss all else, so we are alone united to God. For when the grace of God comes to us, we will be able to do all things. But if we turn from that grace, we will become poor and weak and troubled. Do not be cast down nor in despair, but rest with a calm mind on the will of God. May we bear all things that come to us, all the while praising Jesus Christ. For after winter comes summer; after night returns day; and after the tempest, a great calm.

Book 2 Chapter 8

9

ON LOVING JESUS
ABOVE ALL THINGS

"If you love your father or mother more than you love me,
you are not worthy of being mine;
or if you love your son or daughter more than me,
you are not worthy of being mine."

Matthew 10:37

The Disciple

Blessed are those who understand what it is to love Jesus
and humble themselves for his sake. They must give up all
that they love for their Beloved, for Jesus will not be loved
unless above all things. The love of created things is deceiving and unstable, but the love of Jesus is faithful and lasting.
Those who cling to created things will fall on their slip-
pery foundation, but those who embrace Jesus will stand
upright forever. Let us love him and cling to him as our
closest friend, for he will not forsake us when all others
depart from us, nor will he allow us to perish at the last day.

One day, we will be separated from family and friends—whether we wish it or not—but we will *never* be separated from Christ.

So, we must embrace him in life and death while we commit ourselves to his faithfulness. When all others fail us, he alone is able to help us. Our Beloved, by his very nature, will allow no rival, but alone desires to possess our hearts as a king would sit upon his own throne. If we will refuse to trust in any and every created thing, Jesus will freely take up his home with us. We will find all trust in humans is misplaced, but we can completely rely on the trustworthiness of Jesus.

We will be quickly deceived if we look only on the outward appearance of people, for if we seek our comfort and profit in others, we will too often experience loss. If we seek Jesus in all things, we will certainly find Jesus. But if we seek ourselves, we will also find ourselves—but to our own hurt. For if people do not seek Jesus, they are more hurtful to themselves than all the world and all their enemies.

Book 2 Chapter 7

10

ON OUR UNWORTHINESS
OF CHRIST'S LOVE

Even though God has the right to show his anger and his power, he is very patient with those on whom his anger falls, who are destined for destruction. He does this to make the riches of his glory shine even brighter on those to whom he shows mercy, who were prepared in advance for glory.

Romans 9:22-23

The Disciple

O Lord, I am not worthy of your comfort nor any sense of your presence. You would have dealt justly with me if you had left me poor and deserted. For if I were able to pour forth tears like the sea, I would still not be worthy of your comfort. So, I am not worthy of anything but to be punished because many times I have offended you and in many ways sinned greatly. So, if I received what I deserve, I would not be worthy of even the least of your comforts or help. But the gracious and merciful God makes "the riches of his glory shine even brighter on those to whom he shows mercy, who were prepared in advance for glory" (Romans 9:23).

What have I done, O Lord, that you should sprinkle any heavenly comfort on me? I remember no good that I have done, but I have been ever prone to sin and slow to repentance. It is true, and I cannot deny it. If I should say otherwise, you would rise up against me, and there would be none to defend me. What have I deserved for my sins but hell and everlasting fire? Truly, I confess that I am worthy of all scorn and contempt. And it is not just that I should be considered one of your faithful servants. And although I hate to admit this, but for the sake of truth, I will accuse myself of my sins so that I may receive your mercy.

What will I say, guilty as I am and filled with confusion? I have no words to speak, but this alone: I have sinned, Lord, I have sinned. Have mercy on me. Forgive me. "I have only a few days left, so leave me alone, that I may have a moment of comfort before I leave—never to return—for the land of darkness and utter gloom" (Job 10:20-21).

But what do you require of guilty and miserable sinners? That they be sorry and humble themselves for their sin. Only in true sorrow and humiliation of heart do we hope for pardon, for our troubled conscience to be reconciled, for lost grace to be recovered, and for a soul preserved from the wrath to come to you. For God and the repentant soul will meet each other with a holy kiss (Psalm 85:10).

The humble confession and repentance of sinners is an acceptable sacrifice to you, O Lord, sending forth a smell far sweeter to your nose than fragrant incense. This also is the pleasant ointment that was poured on your sacred feet. "The sacrifice you desire is a broken spirit. You will not reject a broken and repentant heart, O God" (Psalm 51:17). Then we are transformed from a prodigal child worthy of contempt to a welcomed son or daughter. "And while he was still a long way off, his father saw him coming. Filled with love and compassion, he ran to his son, embraced him, and kissed him" (Luke 15:20).

Book 3 Chapter 52

11

ON FLEEING FROM FUTILE HOPE AND PRIDE

We fix our gaze on things that cannot be seen.
For the things we see now will soon be gone,
but the things we cannot see will last forever.

2 Corinthians 4:18

The Disciple

The life of people, who put their trust in other people or any created thing, is futile! By the love of Jesus Christ, we do not need to be afraid or ashamed to be the servant of others and be considered poor in this life. Don't depend upon yourself, but put your hope in God. Do what you can, and God will help your good intentions. Don't trust in your learning nor in the cleverness of others, but trust in the grace of God, who "opposes the proud but gives grace to the humble" (James 4:6).

Let us not boast in our riches if we have them nor in our friends if they are powerful, but boast in God who provides all we need. More than that, he gives himself to those who desire him. We must not be proud of our bodies' strength, because a small germ can make us sick or kill us. Let us not be vain about our skillfulness or abilities, but fear that we will displease our Creator from whom every good gift we have comes.

And we should not count ourselves better than others, for perhaps we may appear worse in the sight of God who knows what is in our souls. Do not be proud of good works, because God does not judge as people do. What pleases people often displeases him. If we regard ourselves good, we should consider others better, so we may maintain our humility. It does us no harm to place ourselves below all others, but great harm occurs when we place ourselves above even one person. Peace is always with the humble person, but in the heart of the proud there is envy and continual wrath.

Book 1 Chapter 7

12

ON HOW SELFISH LOVE HINDERS US

But as I looked at everything I had worked
so hard to accomplish, it was all
so meaningless—like chasing the wind.
There was nothing really worthwhile anywhere.

Ecclesiastes 2:11

The Christ

My friend, you must give all for all and be nothing of your own. Know that the love of yourself is more hurtful to you than anything in the world. According to the love and attitudes which you have, everything more or less clings to you. If you love, be pure, sincere, and well-behaved so you will not be in captivity to anything. Don't covet what you may not have. Do not hold onto anything that holds you back or robs you of inward freedom. How strange it is that you don't commit yourself to me from the very bottom of your heart with everything you have or desire.

43

Why are you consumed with futile sorrow? Why are you weighed down and wearied with unnecessary cares? Desire my good pleasure, and you will suffer no loss. If you seek after this or that, and go here or there according to what seems advantageous to you or what fulfills your own pleasure, you will never be at peace nor free from care. In everything something will be found lacking, and everywhere there will be somebody who opposes you.

Therefore it is not gaining or multiplying of this or that thing which brings you satisfaction but rather the despising of it and cutting it by the root out of your heart. You must understand the worthlessness of money and riches. You must not chase after honor and fickle praise. These things all pass away with the world, and they bring no joy if the spirit of devotion is missing. Neither will you experience peace if it is sought from anyone or anything but God. If you do not live in me, your life is without true foundation. You can change without me, but you cannot *better* yourself without me.

The Disciple

Strengthen me, O God, by the grace of your Holy Spirit. Give me discipline to be strengthened with power in my inner person. Free my heart from all care and trouble, so I may not be drawn away by various desires after anything with little value or great. But may I look on all things as passing away and myself as passing away with them, because there is no profit under the sun, and all is futile and troubling to your spirit. "But as I looked at everything I had worked so hard to accomplish, it was all so meaningless—like chasing the wind. There was nothing really worthwhile anywhere" (Ecclesiastes 2:11). Oh how wise are those who understand this!

Give me, Lord, heavenly wisdom, that I may learn to seek you above all things and to find you. Help me desire you above all things. May I love you. Grant me, according to your wisdom, to accurately understand things as they truly are. Help me to wisely avoid the flatterer and patiently to bear with the one who opposes me. It is great wisdom, not to be carried by every wind of words, nor to give ear to the wicked flattering seductress. With this mindset, we go safely on in your way, Lord.

Book 3 Chapter 27

13

ON WORKS OF CHARITY

*"Then these righteous ones will reply, 'Lord, when did we
ever see you hungry and feed you? Or thirsty and
give you something to drink? Or a stranger and show you
hospitality? Or naked and give you clothing?
When did we ever see you sick or in prison and visit you?'
"And the King will say, 'I tell you the truth,
when you did it to one of the least of these
my brothers and sisters, you were doing it to me!'"*

Matthew 25:37-40

The Disciple

Nothing evil should be done even for some perceived
worldly good or the supposed love for a person. Sometimes
a good work for someone who is suffering must be post-
poned or be revised for the better. So, the good work is not
undone but made better. Without love, no work is beneficial. But whatever is done in charity—no matter how small
or unheralded—will bring forth good fruit. For God knows

what each person is able to do rather than the greatness of what is done.

The one who does much loves much. The one who does much does well. Those who do well serve the public good rather than their own interests. But often what seems to be charity is actually selfish and sinful because it springs from natural motivation, self-will, hope of repayment, or desire of gain or fame.

People who have true and perfect charity, don't seek their own good but desire that God alone is fully glorified. They envy no one, because they seek no selfish joy; nor do they desire to rejoice in themselves. They long to be blessed by God as the highest good. They credit good to no one or no thing except God alone. He is the Fountain from which all good flows, and the End, the Peace, the Joy of all saints. Anyone who has just a spark of true love has learned that all worldly things are full of vanity.

Book 1 Chapter 15

14

ON WALKING IN TRUTH
AND HUMILITY

*O people, the L*ORD *has told you what is good,*
and this is what he requires of you: to do what is right,
to love mercy, and to walk humbly with your God.

Micah 6:8

The Christ

My friend, walk before me in truth. Seek me in the simplicity of your heart. People who walk before me in the truth will be safe from evil attacks, and the truth will deliver them from the schemes and insults of the wicked. If the truth makes you free, you will be free indeed, for you will not care for the vain words of others.

The Disciple

Lord, what you say is true. I pray it is so with me. Let your truth teach me, let it keep me and preserve me safe to the end. Let it free me from all strong and evil desires, and I will walk before you in freedom of heart.

The Christ

I, who am Truth, will teach you the things that are right and pleasing before me. Think on your sins with great displeasure and sorrow. Never think more of yourself because of your good works. Truly, you are a sinner, susceptible to many passions—trapped and bound by them. If you do not guard your heart, you will quickly fall, quickly be conquered, quickly disturbed, and quickly undone. You have no basis for glory, but for many reasons you should consider yourself sinful, for you are far weaker than you are able to admit or comprehend.

Let, therefore, nothing you do be thought of as great. Let nothing be grand, nothing of value or beauty, nothing worthy of honor, nothing lofty, nothing praiseworthy or desirable except that which is eternal. Let the eternal truth please you above all things; let your own great sinfulness continually displease you. Fear, denounce, and flee nothing so much as your own faults and sins, which ought to be more displeasing to you than any loss of goods. There are some who do not walk sincerely before me, but are led by curiosity and pride. They desire to understand the deep things of God, while they neglect themselves and their salvation. These people often fall into great temptations and sins because of their pride and curiosity, for I am against them.

Fear the judgments of God; fear greatly the wrath of the Almighty. Shrink from debating on the works of the Most High, but search carefully your own shortcomings and consider the sins from which you have fallen, and the many good things you have neglected. There are some who carry their devotion only in books, some in pictures, some in outward signs and figures. Some have much of me on their lips, but little of me in their hearts. But others, who have been enlightened in their understanding and purged in their affections, continually long after eternal things, hear of earthly things with unwillingness, and reluctantly meet their bodily needs. These friends of mine understand what the Spirit of truth speaks to them, for he teaches them to despise earthly things and to love heavenly things, to neglect the world, and to desire heaven all the day and night.

Book 3 Chapter 4

15

ON THE INWARD VOICE
OF CHRIST

*When the Spirit of truth comes, he will guide you
into all truth. He will not speak on his own but will
tell you what he has heard. . . . He will bring me glory
by telling you whatever he receives from me.*

John 16:13-14

The Disciple

"I listen carefully to what God the LORD is saying, for he
speaks peace to his faithful people. But let them not return
to their foolish ways" (Psalm 85:8). Blessed is the soul who
hears the Lord speaking and receives the word of comfort
from his mouth. Blessed are the ears that receive the echoes
of the soft whisper of God and aren't distracted by the
murmurings of this world. Truly blessed are the ears that
listen—not to the sounds surrounding them—but to the
voice of Truth inside. Blessed are the eyes that are closed to
outward things, but are focused on things within. Blessed

51

are they who search inward things and study to prepare themselves by daily exercises for the receiving of heavenly mysteries. Blessed are they who long to have time for God and free themselves from every time-waster in the world. Think on these things, O my soul. Shut the doors of your selfish and sinful desires so you may hear what the Lord God will say within you.

Jesus, our Beloved, teaches, "I am your salvation. I am your peace and your life. Remain faithful to me and you will find peace." Put away all earthly, temporary things. Seek after things that are eternal. For what are temporal things but deceptive illusions? How can any created thing help you if you have abandoned your Creator? So, don't depend on created things. Put them away and fully give yourself to the Creator. Be obedient and faithful to him, that you may gain true blessedness.

Book 3 Chapter 1

16

ON TRUTH WITHOUT
THE NOISE OF WORDS

---

*Your own ears will hear him. Right behind you
a voice will say, "This is the way you should go,"
whether to the right or to the left.*

Isaiah 30:21

The Disciple

"Speak, Lord, your servant is listening" (1 Samuel 3:9). I
am your servant. "Give discernment to me, your servant;
then I will understand your laws" (Psalm 119:125). Incline
my heart to the words of your mouth. Distill your words as
dew. In earlier times, the children of Israel spoke to Moses
"You speak to us, and we will listen. But don't let God speak
directly to us, or we will die!" (Exodus 20:19). I do not
pray this way, but rather with Samuel the prophet. I beg
you humbly and earnestly, "Speak, Lord, for your servant
listens." Don't let Moses speak to me, nor any prophet, but
rather speak to me, Lord, who inspired and illuminated

all the prophets. Not the prophets, but you alone, can perfectly fill me with knowledge.

Prophets indeed can give us words, but they cannot give the Spirit. They speak with great beauty, but they do not burn in my heart when you are silent. They give us scriptures, but only you give understanding to them. They bring us mysteries, but you reveal the things which are significant. They pronounce commandments, but only you give me power to obey them. They show the way, but only you give strength for the journey. They speak to my outward actions, but only you instruct and enlighten my heart. They water, but you produce the harvest. They cry out with words, but only you give understanding to the hearer.

Therefore don't let Moses speak to me, but only you, O Lord my God, Eternal Truth. Without your words, I die and bring forth no fruit, being outwardly admonished, but not changed within. May I not only hear the Word but follow it. May it not be simply known but loved; not just believed but obeyed, so I may not be judged. Speak, Lord, for your servant listens. "You have the words that give eternal life" (John 6:68). Speak to me for the comfort of my soul, for the transformation of my whole life, and for the praise, glory, and eternal honor of your name.

Book 3 Chapter 2

17

ON HOW TO HEAR
THE WORDS OF GOD

"The Spirit alone gives eternal life.
Human effort accomplishes nothing. And the very words
I have spoken to you are spirit and life."

John 6:63

The Christ

My friend, hear my words, for they are most satisfying,
surpassing all the knowledge of the philosophers and wise
men of this world. My words are spirit. "The very words I
have spoken to you are spirit and life" (John 6:63). They are
not judged by human understanding. They are not spoken
to impress others, but to be heard in silence and received
with all humility and deep love.

The Disciple

Blessed, O Lord, is the person whom you teach and instruct
in your law, that you give rest in times of trouble. "When

doubts filled my mind, your comfort gave me renewed hope and cheer" (Psalm 94:19). I will not feel abandoned on this earth.

The Christ

I taught the prophets from the beginning. Even now, I continue to speak to those who are deaf and hard of hearing toward my voice. Many love to listen to the world rather than to God. They follow after their human desires more eagerly than after the good pleasure of God. The world promises things that are small and temporary—and people respond enthusiastically. I promise things that are great and eternal, and the hearts of mortal humans are slow to respond. Who are those who serve and obey me in all things with the same care in which they serve the world and its rulers?

For a little reward, people make a long journey; for eternal life many will scarcely lift a foot off the ground. They seek poor rewards of money in their shameful strife. For a trivial promise, people will work day and night.

What shame for those who strive for such worthless rewards while ignoring eternal goods, my infinite rewards, and heaven's highest honors. For fading glory, they reject eternal glory that does not fade away. It is annoying for them to work even a little. So, be ashamed lazy and discontented servant, for you are readier for death than life. They rejoice more heartily in worthless things than in the truth. Sometimes, indeed, their hopes are disappointed, but my promises never fail, and I never send away anyone who trusts in me. What I have promised I will give; what I have said I will fulfill—but only to a person who remains faithful in my love to the very end. So, I am the rewarder of all good people and a strong supporter of all who are godly.

Write my words in your heart and diligently consider them, for they will be very helpful to you in times of temptation. What do you not understand when you read? I will make myself known with my presence. I will be with you in times of temptation and comfort. I will teach you each in these two situations: convicting you of short-comings and encouraging you to grow by grace. If you have my words and do not reject them, no one will judge you in the day of judgment.

The Disciple

O Lord my God, you are all that is good within me; who am I that I should dare speak to you? I am the least of your servants. I am the very poorest of your servants, a miserable worm, much poorer and more despicable than I know or dare to say. Nevertheless remember, O Lord, that I am nothing. I have nothing, and can do nothing. Only you are good and holy. You can do all things; you are over all things, fill all things, and leave only the sinner empty. Remember your tender mercies and fill my heart with your grace. Your work is always accomplished.

How can I bear up under this miserable life unless your mercy and grace strengthen me? Do not turn your face from me or delay your coming. Do not withdraw your comfort from me for fear that my soul will gasp after you as a thirsty land. Lord, teach me to do your will, teach me to walk humbly and uprightly before you. You are my wisdom. You are my truth. You have known me before the world was made.

Book 3 Chapter 3

18

ON THE KNOWLEDGE
OF TRUTH

*Jesus said to the people who believed in him,
"You are truly my disciples if you remain faithful
to my teachings. And you will know the truth,
and the truth will set you free."*

John 8:31-32

The Disciple

Happy is the person who is taught by Truth itself, not by
unreliable words. Our own judgment and feelings often
deceive us, and we understand only a little of the truth.
What is the benefit to argue about hidden and mysterious
things that we will not be judged for not knowing? Oh,
what foolishness to neglect the things which are profitable
and necessary and to give our minds to things which are
curious and hurtful. We have eyes, but we do not see.

The more people have unity and simplicity in themselves, the greater and deeper things they understand. It

is not by human labor, but we receive the light of understanding from above. The spirit which is pure, sincere, and steadfast is not distracted though it has many things to do, because it does all things to the honor of God. It strives to be free from self-seeking thoughts. What is more of a hindrance and annoyance to us than our own undisciplined hearts? People who are good and devout plan beforehand—within their own hearts—what they will do. So, they are not drawn away by the evil desires of their will, but subject everything to the judgment of right reason. Who has a harder battle to fight than the one who strives for self-mastery? And this should be our goal: to master ourselves and, thus, daily grow stronger than our own selves and go into holy completeness.

All perfection in this life has some imperfection mixed in with it. All our power of sight is not without some darkness. A humble knowledge of ourselves is a surer way to God than the deep searching for human wisdom. Not that learning or careful consideration of something is bad, but a good conscience and a holy life are better than all. Many who seek knowledge rather than good living go astray and bear little or no fruit.

If only we would give the same diligence to the rooting out of vice and the planting of virtue as we give to futile questionings. At the Day of Judgment, we will be not be questioned as to what we have read, but what we have done; not how well we have spoken, but how holy we have lived.

The glory of the world quickly passes away! Oh that we learned people would have had our life and knowledge agree with each other. Only then would what we would have read and studied result in a good purpose. How many perish through empty learning in the world while caring so little about serving God? And because they love to be great, rather than to be humble, "their minds became dark and confused" (Romans 1:21). People are only truly great when they have great love, when they consider themselves small and count all heights of honor as nothing. And if we are truly learned, we will do the will of God and forsake our own wisdom.

Book 1 Chapter 3

19

ON WISDOM IN ACTION

Dear friends, do not believe everyone who claims
to speak by the Spirit. You must test them to see
if the spirit they have comes from God.
For there are many false prophets in the world.

1 John 4:1

The Disciple

You must not trust every word of others or feelings within yourselves, but cautiously and patiently ask if the matter is godly. Unhappily, we are so weak that we find it easier to believe and speak evil of others, rather than their good. But Christ-like people do not pay attention to every bit of news, because they know that in human weakness they are prone to evil and untruthful words.

This is great wisdom for us: do not to be hasty in our actions or stubborn in our own opinions. A part of this wisdom also is not to believe every word we hear, nor to tell others all that we hear, nor even though we believe it.

Take advice from a person who is wise and has a good conscience. Let us seek to learn from one wiser than ourselves rather than follow our own imaginations. A good life makes us wise toward God and gives us experience in many things. The more humble we are and the more obedient we are toward God, the wiser we will be in all things, and the more our souls will be at peace.

Book 1 Chapter 4

20

ON AVOIDING RASH JUDGMENT

"Do not judge others, and you will not be judged.
For you will be treated as you treat others.
The standard you use in judging is the standard
by which you will be judged."

Matthew 7:1-2

The Disciple

We must beware of judging others, but first look to our-selves. People who judge are engaged in futile labor and often make errors. They easily fall into sin. But if we judge and examine ourselves, that always works for a good purpose. However, by judging based on our own personal likes and dislikes, it is difficult to make true and godly judgments. If God was always our only desire, we would be less troubled and make fewer poor judgments.

But often some secret thought lurking within us or some outward circumstance turns us from God's path. Many are secretly seeking their own desires—and do not even know it. They seem to enjoy peace of mind—as long as things go well and their desires are met. But if their desires are frustrated and broken, immediately they are shaken and displeased. Differing feelings and opinions very often bring about dissensions between friends, citizens, members of different faiths, and godly people.

Our own customs and habits are not easily given up, and it is not easy to see from another's point of view. If we depend more on our own reason or experience than upon the power of Jesus Christ, true discernment will come slowly with much difficulty. God wants us to be perfectly obedient to himself. Then all our reason will be revealed by abundant love toward him and others.

Book 1 Chapter 14

21

ON NOT BELIEVING EVERYONE

"Beware of false prophets who come disguised as harmless sheep but are really vicious wolves. You can identify them by their fruit, that is, by the way they act."

Matthew 7:15-16

The Disciple

"Oh, please help us against our enemies, for all human help is useless" (Psalm 60:11). How often have I failed to find faithfulness where I thought I would find it? How many times have I found it where I least expected it? So, hope in people is futile. But the salvation of the just, O God, is in you. Blessed be you, O Lord my God, in all things which happen unto us. We are weak and unstable. We are quickly deceived and changed for the worse.

Who are people who are able to keep themselves aware and conscious of their surroundings so they do not fall into the trap of perplexity? Those who trust in you, O Lord, and seek you with a pure heart. They do not so easily slip.

And if they fall into and are entangled by any trouble, you quickly deliver them. You comfort them, because you will not forsake those who trust you to the end. A friend who continues to be faithful in all trouble is a rare find. You, O Lord, are most faithful in all things. There is no other one but you.

Oh, how truly wise is the holy soul who can say, "My mind is steadfastly fixed, and it is grounded in Christ." If it were so, the fear of humans would not easily tempt me nor would critical words harm me.

Who is able to see all things in the future, who can guard against all future ills? If even things which are expected sometimes hurt us, what can things which are not foreseen do but seriously injure? Why have I not provided better for my miserable self? Why, also, have I blindly followed others? We are frail, fallen people, even though we are God's creations.

Whom will I trust, O Lord? Whom will I trust but you? You are Truth. You do not deceive, nor can you be deceived. But on the other hand, every person is a liar, unstable, and weak—especially in his or her words. So, we should rarely believe what seems right at face value.

With wisdom, you have previously warned us to beware of people: "'If anyone tells you, "Look, here is the Messiah," or "There he is," don't believe it'" (Matthew 24:23). I have been taught by my own losses that I should be more careful and less foolish. "Be cautious," some say. "Be cautious and keep to yourself what I tell you." But, while I am silent about the matter, that person can't keep silent about it. He immediately betrays me and himself as he spreads the secret. Protect me, O Lord, from such mischief-making and reckless people. Don't let me fall into their hands—and don't let me ever do such things myself. Put true and dependable words into my mouth, and remove a deceitful tongue far from me. What I would not want others doing to hurt me, may I not do it to others.

It is good and peaceable to be silent concerning others and not to carelessly believe all that is said. It is good to open ourselves up to only a trusted few. Protect my heart, and may I not be blown about with every wind of words. May I desire that everything I do inwardly and outwardly be done according to your good will and pleasure. To be spiritually safe, you must not seek human approval and desire the things which earn admiration in the world. In all sincerity, seek to conform to God's priorities and heavenly perspective. Too many have been hurt spiritually by their good works being publicized and hastily praised. How truly beneficial it is to preserve God's grace by remaining silent and avoiding the world's temptations and warfare.

Book 3 Chapter 45

22

ON HOPE AND TRUST
IN GOD ALONE

Let all that I am wait quietly before God,
for my hope is in him. He alone is my rock and
my salvation, my fortress where I will not be shaken.
My victory and honor come from God alone.
He is my refuge, a rock where no enemy can reach me.

Psalm 62:5-7

The Disciple

O Lord, what trust do I have in this life? What is my greatest comfort of all the things which are seen under heaven? Is it not you, O Lord my God, whose mercies are without number? Have I ever been well without you? And how has evil fled when you are near? I would rather be poor with you than rich without you. I choose to be a pilgrim on earth with you than without you in the heavens. Where you are, there is heaven. And where you are not, there is death and hell. You alone are my desire and, therefore, I must groan and cry out earnestly for you. In short, I depend fully on you—and you alone—to help me in the necessities of life. You are my hope. You are my trust. You are my comforter and most faithful friend in all things.

All people seek their own desires, but you desire my salvation and my good. You work all things to my good (Romans 8:28). Even though I am exposed to many temptations and adversities, you have planned all of this for my good. You want to prove your love to me in a thousand ways. In these temptations and adversities, you should not be loved and praised any less than when you were filling me with heavenly comfort.

In you, therefore, O Lord God, I put all my hope and security. I lay all my trials and anguish upon you, because I find everything and everyone else to be weak and unstable. Without you yourself to assist me, I find no comfort, instruction, or safety. Many friends are not helpful or comforting. Wise counselors do not give useful answers. Books by learned authors do not always console or provide deliverance. Beautiful, secret hideaways do not shelter.

For all things which promise peace and joy are insufficient without you present. So, you are the source of all goodness, fullness of life, and peace in my soul. Hope in you is the strongest comfort for your servants. "I look to you for help, O Sovereign Lord. You are my refuge"

(Psalm 141:8). In you, O God, Father of mercies, I put my complete trust.

Bless and sanctify my soul with heavenly blessing that it may become a holy dwelling for your eternal glory. And let nothing be found in my life which would offend your holiness. According to the greatness of your goodness and many mercies, look upon me and hear the prayer of your unworthy servant, who is far exiled from you in the land of the shadow of death. Protect and preserve the soul of your servant amid so many dangers of corruptible life. By your grace guiding me, direct me to our eternal home of happiness and life. Amen.

Book 3 Chapter 59

23

ON CASTING
ALL CARE UPON GOD

Give all your worries and cares to God,
for he cares about you.

1 Peter 5:7

The Christ

My friend, allow me to do with you what I wish. I know how you view life and what is important from a human perspective. You think and make decisions based on what is beneficial to you right now.

The Disciple

Lord, what you say is true. You care more for me than I care for myself. When I don't cast all my care upon you, I do not stand firm and secure. So, do with me whatever you desire, for I know your purpose cannot be anything but good. I bless and trust you when you leave me in the dark. I bless and trust you when you bring me into the light. I bless and trust you when you comfort me. I bless and trust you when you cause me to be troubled.

The Christ

My friend, even as you desire to walk with me, you must also be willing to both suffer and rejoice. You must be as willing to be poor and needy as you are willing to be full and rich.

The Disciple

Lord, I will willingly bear for you whatever it is you desire to come upon me. Without complaining, I will receive from your hand good and evil, sweet and bitter, joy and sadness. I will give you thanks for all things that happen to me. Keep me from all sin, and I will not fear death or hell. Only do not cast me away forever or erase me from the book of life. Then no troubles and trials which will come upon me will do me any harm.

Book 3 Chapter 17

24

ON COMMITTING OURSELVES INTO GOD'S HANDS

But I am trusting you, O LORD, saying,
"You are my God!" My future is in your hands.

Psalm 31:14-15

The Disciple

O Lord, Holy Father, I bless you now and evermore, because whatever you desire for me will do me good. Let your servant rejoice in you—not in himself, nor in any other—because you alone are my true joy. You are my hope and my reward. You are my joy and my honor, O Lord. What does your servant have that he did not receive from you—and not by his own merit? You are all things which you have made and given to me. "I have been sick and close to death since my youth" (Psalm 88:15). My soul is sorrowful to the point of tears. Sometimes I have been anxious because of the sufferings that have come against my soul.

I long after the joy of peace. I beg for the peace of your children, for in your comfort you feed them. If you give peace or pour out holy joy, the soul of your servant will be full of song and devoted to praise. But if you withdraw the sense of your presence, I will not be able to follow your commandments. Rather I will pound my chest and bow my knees because I cannot sense your presence as before "when [you] lit up the way before me and I walked safely through the darkness (Job 29:3). "Hide me in the shadow of your wings" (Psalm 17:8). Protect me from the temptations that come against me.

O Father, righteous and always worthy of praise, the time is coming when your servant is to be proven faithful. O beloved Father, it is beneficial that at this time, your servant should suffer somewhat for your sake. O Father, forever to be adored, the hour comes that you knew from the beginning of time. For in a little while, your servant will outwardly be struck down, but always live inwardly standing with you. For a little while, I will be disregarded, humbled, and fail in the eyes of my peers. I will be wasted with sufferings and weaknesses, only to rise again with you in the dawn of the new light and be glorified in the heavenly places. O Holy Father, you have planned, desired, and commanded it should be done to me.

For this is your favor to me, that your friend and servant should suffer and be troubled in the world for your love's sake as often and through whatever and whoever you have allowed it to be done. Without your counsel and providence—and without cause—nothing comes to pass on the earth. "My suffering was good for me, for it taught me to pay attention to your decrees" (Psalm 119:71). It cast away all pride of heart and presumption. It was beneficial for me that confusion covered my face, because it caused me to seek you rather than my friends' comfort. But I have also learned to respect your unsearchable judgment, that afflicts the just along with the wicked, but not without equity and justice.

O beloved Father, I am in your hands, I bow myself under your correction and discipline.

Book 3 Chapter 50

25

ON NOT TRUSTING ONESELF

Trust in the LORD with all your heart;
do not depend on your own understanding.

Proverbs 3:5

The Disciple

Because grace and understanding are often lacking in us, we cannot place any confidence in ourselves. There is little light within us, and what we do have we quickly lose by negligence. Often, we don't recognize how great our inward blindness is. We often do wrong and, worse, excuse it. Sometimes we are moved by human passion and count it as godly zeal. We criticize little faults in others and pass over great faults in ourselves. We quickly recognize how people mistreat us, but we don't recognize how much we mistreat others. If we would recognize our own shortcomings, we would be less judgmental of others.

Spiritually-minded people, who diligently consider their own faults, easily keep silent about other people. We will never be spiritually-minded and godly unless we are silent concerning other people's lives and take full responsibility for our own. If we think wholly upon God and our own spiritual lives, we will be affected very little by the lives of those outside our doors. Where are we when we are not aware of our own selves? And when we dwell on our own successes, are we neglecting our spiritual lives? If we want to have peace and true unity with others, we must put aside all others' lives and concentrate on our own spiritual lives.

We will make great progress if we keep ourselves free from temporary cares. Sadly, we will fall away from God if we set our value on any worldly thing. Let nothing be great, nothing high, nothing pleasing, nothing acceptable to us except for God himself or his works. Consider any comfort absolutely useless if it comes from a created thing. The soul that loves God does not look at anything that is beneath God. God alone is eternal and incomprehensible, filling all things: the comfort of the soul and the true joy of the heart.

Book 2 Chapter 5

26

ON TRUSTING GOD
IN HIDDEN MATTERS

He is the Rock; his deeds are perfect.
Everything he does is just and fair. He is a faithful God
who does no wrong; how just and upright he is!

Deuteronomy 32:4

The Christ

My friend, don't argue about the hidden workings of God
that are beyond your comprehension. Do not ask, why is
this person seemingly neglected and this person shown
such great favor? Why is this person greatly afflicted and
this one so highly exalted? These things are beyond human
power of understanding. Divine judgments are beyond
earthly reasoning, arguments, or explanations. So, when the
enemy of our soul—or curious people—ask such questions,
answer with the words of the psalmist: "O LORD, you are
righteous, and your regulations are fair" (Psalm 119:137).
Also answer: "The laws of the LORD are true; each one is

fair" (Psalm 19:9). My judgments are to be feared, not to be disputed, because they are incomprehensible to human understanding.

And don't inquire or dispute about the merits of godly people. Who is holier than another? Who is the greater in the kingdom of heaven? Such questions often create useless strife and contention. They also promote pride and vain glory as well as envy and dissension. One person arrogantly tries to exalt one spiritual leader and another person another leader. To wish to know and search out such things is not fruitful, but displeasing to the very people you wish to exalt. For I am not a God of disorder but of peace (1 Corinthians 14:33). That peace comes not from self-exaltation, but true humility.

All my friends are one through the bond of love, and being united in love, they are of one heart and one mind.

And far better, they love me above themselves and their own merits. For being caught up above themselves and drawn beyond self-love, their priority is *my* love. They rest in me with perfect joy. There is nothing which can turn them away or press them down, for they are full of eternal truth. They burn with the fire of inextinguishable love. So, let all earthly and natural people not criticize the state of my friends, as they do not know anything except to love their own personal enjoyment. They take away and add according to their own inclination, rather than pleasing the eternal truth.

Be careful, my friends, that you don't treat those things which are beyond your knowledge with curiosity, but make it your goal to be found in the kingdom of heaven. Even if you may know those who are holier than others or are considered the greatest in the kingdom of heaven, the most important thing to know is this: Humble yourself before me and I will raise you up to give greater praise to my name. Those who consider how great are their sins, how small their virtues, and how far they are from godly perfection are far more acceptable in the sight of God, than those who dispute about their greatness or smallness.

You will be completely satisfied if you learn to be content and avoid foolish babbling. Do not glory in your own merits, knowing that any goodness in yourself is from me. I, the God of infinite love, have given you these things. Then you will be abundantly filled with my great love, so that no glory or joy is lacking in your life. All my friends, the higher you are exalted in my glory, the more humble you will find yourself. You will be nearer and dearer to me. And so, it is written that my followers will "fall down and worship the one sitting on the throne (the one who lives forever and ever). And they lay their crowns before the throne" (Revelation 4:10). And they will worship me forever and ever.

Book 3 Chapter 58

27

ON TRUSTING GOD FOR NECESSITIES

*"So don't worry about these things, saying,
'What will we eat? What will we drink? What will we
wear?' These things dominate the thoughts of unbelievers,
but your heavenly Father already knows all your needs.
Seek the Kingdom of God above all else, and live righteously,
and he will give you everything you need."*

Matthew 6:31-33

The Disciple

O most sweet and loving Lord, whom I devoutly desire to
receive, you know my weaknesses and my sufferings, my evil
thoughts and actions. I am often weighed down, tempted,
disturbed, and defiled. I come to you for a remedy. I beg
you for comfort and support. I speak to you who knows all
things, to whom all my secrets are open, and to whom alone
is able perfectly to comfort and help me. You know what
good things I need and how poor I am in righteousness.

And so, I stand poor and naked before you, needing grace and praying for mercy. Whet my appetite for righteousness, kindle my coldness with the fire of your love, illuminate my blindness with the brightness of your presence. Turn all earthly things into bitterness for me, all sorrowful and opposing things into patience, all things worthless and created into contempt and nothingness. Lift up my heart to you in heaven, and don't allow me to aimlessly wander over the earth. Be my only satisfaction from this day forward forever, because you alone are my food and drink, my love and joy, my delight, and my whole good.

Please, with your presence, kindle, consume, and transform me into yourself that I may be made one spirit by the grace of unity with you and the refining of your pure love! Don't allow me to go away from you hungry and dry, but deal mercifully with me, as you have dealt with your children in the past. I marvel that you are a fire always burning and never failing, love purifying the heart and enlightening the understanding.

Book 4 Chapter 16

28

ON THE PURPOSE
OF ADVERSITY

Dear brothers and sisters, when troubles of any kind
come your way, consider it an opportunity for great joy.
For you know that when your faith is tested,
your endurance has a chance to grow. So let it grow,
for when your endurance is fully developed, you will be
perfect and complete, needing nothing.

James 1:2-4

The Disciple

It is good for us that we sometimes have sorrows and
adversities, for they often make us realize we are only strangers and sojourners on this earth and that we can't put our
trust in worldly things. It is good that we sometimes endure
opposition and are judged unfairly. When we experience
this trouble, it is for our good. For these things help us to be
humble and shield us from conceit. For when people speak

evil against us falsely and give us no credit for good, then we seek more earnestly the approval of God.

So, we need to rest wholly upon God, rather than needing to seek comfort from the hands of people. When people who fear God are afflicted, tried, or oppressed with evil thoughts, they realize how much they need him, since without him they can do no good thing. Then those with heavy hearts, groan and cry out from the trouble heart. There are even times when God's children grow weary of life and desire to depart and be with Christ. All this teaches them that on earth there is no perfect security or fullness of peace.

Book 1 Chapter 12

29

ON HUMAN MISERY

I once thought . . . things were valuable, but now
I consider them worthless because of what Christ has done.
Yes, everything else is worthless when compared with the
infinite value of knowing Christ Jesus my Lord. For his sake
I have discarded everything else, counting it all as garbage,
so that I could gain Christ and become one with him.

Philippians 3:7-9

The Disciple

Unless we turn to God, we will be miserable wherever and with whomever we find ourselves. We become anxious because things don't happen according to our wishes and desires. But who has everything according to his or her own wishes? Neither I nor you nor any person on earth. There is no one free from trouble; not even the king or pope. Who is the one who is the happiest? The one whom God gives the strength to suffer.

Many foolish and unstable people say, "See what a prosperous life that person has. How great, powerful, and exalted." But lift up your eyes to the good things of heaven, and you will see that all these worldly things are nothing. They are utterly undependable and even wearisome, because they are never possessed without trouble and fear. Our happiness does not lie in the accumulation of temporary things, but in being content with a modest portion. The more we desire to be spiritual, the more wretched and bitter the present life seems, because the more clearly we see the defects of human corruption. For to eat, drink, watch, sleep, rest, labor, and be subject to the other necessities of nature, is truly a great inconvenience and burden to a devout people who desire to be released and free from all sin.

For the inner person is heavily burdened with the necessities of the body in this world. And so, the psalmist devoutly prayed to be free from them, saying, "My problems go from bad to worse. Oh, save me from them all!" (Psalm 25:17). But woe to those who do not recognize their own misery, and an even greater woe to those who love this miserable and corruptible life. Some people go so far that if they might live here always, they would care nothing for the kingdom of God.

Oh foolish and faithless of heart are those people buried so deeply in worldly things that they desire nothing except the things of the flesh! Miserable ones! Too sadly at last, they will learn how sinful and worthless were the things of earth they loved. The saints of God and all loyal friends of Christ, consider things which please the flesh or flourish in this life as nothing, and desire with their whole hope and affection things which are above. Their whole desire is directed upwards to everlasting and invisible things, lest they should be drawn downwards by the love of things visible.

Children, we must not lose our desire to grow and develop spiritually. There is still time; the hour is not past. Let us not put off our resolution. Get up and begin this very moment. Say, "Now is the time to do, to fight, and the right time to change my life." When we are ill at ease and troubled, that is the time when we are closest to blessing. We must go through fire and water before God may bring us into a safe place. Unless we forcefully discipline ourselves, we will not conquer our faults. So long as we carry about with us this frail body, we cannot be without sin, nor can we live without weariness and trouble. Gladly would we enjoy rest from all misery. But because, through sin, we have lost innocence, we have also lost true happiness.

Therefore we must be patient and wait for the mercy of God, until this tyranny is past and our earthly life is swallowed up in eternal life.

O how great is our weakness, for we are ever prone to evil! Today we confess our sin and tomorrow we commit the very same sin that we confessed yesterday. We resolve to avoid a fault and within an hour we have committed the fault as if we never resolved at all. So, we have good reason to humble ourselves and never to think highly of ourselves knowing that we are so weak and undisciplined. How quickly some virtue is lost by our negligence—after we have worked hard to attain it through grace.

What will become of us at the end if at the beginning we are uncommitted and idle? Woe to us if we choose to rest, as though it were a time of peace and security, and do not strive and struggle for a life of true holiness. Rather, we need to start afresh and be instructed in good living if we hope for transformation and spiritual maturity.

Book 1 Chapter 22

30

ON OUR WEAKNESSES

---

*We are pressed on every side by troubles, but we are not
crushed. We are perplexed, but not driven to despair.
We are hunted down, but never abandoned by God.
We get knocked down, but we are not destroyed.
Through suffering, our bodies continue to share
in the death of Jesus so that the life of Jesus
may also be seen in our bodies.*

2 Corinthians 4:8-10

The Disciple

"Finally, I confessed all my sins to you and stopped trying
to hide my guilt" (Psalm 32:5). Often a small thing casts me
down and makes me sad. I resolve that I will act bravely, but
when a little temptation comes, immediately I am in a great
conflict. It's often a very small matter through which a very
great temptation comes. And whenever I imagine myself
safe for even a moment, when I am not on guard, a little
puff of wind will nearly overcome me.

O Lord, my humility and my frailty are completely known to you. Be merciful to me and lift "me out of the pit of despair, out of the mud and the mire" (Psalm 40:2). Don't let me remain cast down. This is what throws me backward in my spiritual journey and confuses me. I fall so easily, and am so weak in resisting my temptations. And though temptation's assault is not according to your plan, it is violent and sorrowful. This daily conflict wears me down. I am made aware of my infirmities when hateful, sinful thoughts rush in far more easily than they depart.

Oh most mighty God of Israel, lover of all your faithful children, please look upon my labor and sorrow. Give me strength in all these struggles. Strengthen me with heavenly determination, so that my fleshly desires do not overpower my spirit. Rule over me, Father, so I can strive victoriously over the temptations of this most miserable life. Oh, what a life is this, where troubles and trials and miseries never cease, where all things are full of traps and enemies. For as one trouble or temptation leaves, another comes. Even while the former conflict is still raging, numerous more come unexpectedly.

And how can this earth be loved, seeing that it is filled with so many bitter things, mishaps, and miseries? How can it be even called life, when it produces so many deaths and plagues? Even though the world is criticized, because it is deceitful and vain, nevertheless it is not easily given up, because the desires of the flesh have too much rule over it. Some draw us to love, some to hate. The lust of the flesh, the lust of the eyes, and the pride of life, draw us to love the world; but the punishments and miseries which righteously follow these things, bring forth hatred of the world and weariness.

Evil desires "sound like animals howling among the bushes, huddled together beneath the nettles" (Job 30:7). They do not savor or even perceive the delight of God nor the inward gracefulness of virtue. But those who completely despise the world and strive to live unto God in holy discipline are not ignorant of the divine delight promised to all who truly deny themselves and see clearly how sadly the world errs and in how many ways it deceives its inhabitants.

Book 3 Chapter 20

31

ON THE LACK OF
ALL COMFORT

I have learned how to be content with whatever I have.
I know how to live on almost nothing or with everything.
I have learned the secret of living in every situation,
whether it is with a full stomach or empty,
with plenty or little. For I can do everything
through Christ, who gives me strength.

Philippians 4:11-13

The Disciple

It is not hard to despise human comfort when God is present. But, it is a great thing—a very great thing—to be able to bear the loss of both human and divine comfort and, for the love of God, to willingly seek no comfort or to feel no righteousness. It's not a great matter if we are faithful and cheerful when blessings come our way. We can all rejoice then. We ride high when the grace of God carries us.

And how marvelous to feel no burden, but to be carried by the Almighty and led onward by the Spirit from on high.

We are willing to trade anything for comfort, and it is difficult for people to be freed from themselves. But Lawrence of Rome and the bishop of Rome, Sixtus, were both martyred, and overcame the love of the world, despising every created thing. So, by the love of their Creator, they also overcame the love of people. Instead of human comfort, they chose God's good pleasure. Like them, we must also learn to love God more than any beloved friends or spiritual leaders. And even if we are deserted by friends, it reminds us that we will all be parted from one another in the end.

We must strive hard and long against ourselves to give ourselves completely to God and to direct all our love toward God. It is too easy for people to depend solely on other people. But a true lover of Christ, and a diligent seeker after righteousness, does not fall back upon human comforts nor earthly pleasures that can be touched and tasted. The Christ-follower desires hard discipline and severe labor to become like his master.

When spiritual comfort is given by God, let us receive it with thanks, and realize it is the gift of God, not our own handiwork. We must not be proud, selfishly rejoice, or foolishly credit ourselves, but humbly receive comfort as a gift and be cautious and careful in all we do. For this time of rejoicing will pass away—and temptation *will* follow. When comfort is taken from us, don't immediately despair, but wait with humility and patience for Christ's heavenly presence. God is able to give us back even greater favor and comfort. This is not new nor strange to those who have faced trial on God's path. For the great saints and ancient prophets were transformed through trials.

The psalmist writes, "When I was prosperous, I said, 'Nothing can stop me now!' Your favor, O LORD, made me as secure as a mountain" (Psalm 30:6-7). He goes on to write what he felt when the favor departed: "Then you turned away from me, and I was shattered. I cried out to you, O LORD. I begged the Lord for mercy" (Psalm 30:7-8). When God heard his prayer and had mercy on the psalmist, he testified, "You have turned my mourning into joyful dancing. You have taken away my clothes of mourning and clothed me with joy" (Psalm 30:11). If it was so with the great saints, we who are poor don't need to despair if we are sometimes warm and sometimes in the cold. The Spirit comes and goes according to the good pleasure of his will. Even the righteous Job said, "For you examine us every morning and test us every moment" (Job 7:18).

On what can we hope and in what can we trust except in the great mercy of God and the hope of heavenly grace? There is little help in good people, faithful friends, holy books, inspiring messages, or sweet hymns and songs when we feel deserted by God's favor and left to our own poverty. There is no better remedy than patience, denial of self, and obeying his commandments.

I have never found any people so religious and godly, that they haven't felt a withdrawal of divine favor and lack of passion. No saints were ever so filled with ecstasy or so enlightened, but that sooner or later they were tempted. For one is not worthy of the great vision of God who has not been tested by some temptation. For temptation often precedes divine comfort which will follow, for it is promised to those who have been proved faithful by temptation: "To everyone who is victorious I will give fruit from the tree of life in the paradise of God" (Revelation 2:7).

Divine comfort is given so that a person may be stronger to bear hardship. And temptation follows so we will not become proud in the blessings of God. The devil doesn't sleep. You physical desires are not yet dead. So, always be ready for battle, because enemies stand on your right and left, and they are never at rest.

Book 2 Chapter 9

32

ON BEARING INJURIES

Together with Christ we are heirs of God's glory.
But if we are to share his glory, we must also share
his suffering. Yet what we suffer now is nothing
compared to the glory he will reveal to us later.

Romans 8:17-18

The Christ

My friend, stop complaining and consider my own and
my followers' suffering. "After all, you have not yet given
your lives in your struggle against sin" (Hebrews 12:4).
You have suffered little compared to those who have suffered so many things and have been so strongly tempted.
You have suffered very little in comparison to those who
have suffered such terrible troubles. They were tempted and tried in many ways. You ought to remember the
horrible sufferings of others so you might bear the lesser
ones more easily. And if they don't seem little, make sure
it was not your impatience that caused these troubles. But

whether they be little or great, determine to bear them with patience.

So, determine to bear suffering patiently. If you do this, you are wise and deserve praise. You will find that if you have this attitude and behavior, you will bear trouble easier. However, do not say, "I will patiently endure this person's actions, but I cannot bear the things that person has done to me, for he has done terrible and unimaginable harm." This is a foolish thought. It is not patient suffering if it is conditioned by the person or offenses against you.

Impatient people will only bear those things that seem justified or committed by a pleasing person. But the truly patient person does not take into consideration if the trying person is superior, inferior, or equal to him, whether the offender is a good and holy person, or a perverse and worthless individual. Truly patient people are indifferent as to who has hurt them. They gratefully accept all from the hand of God and count it great gain. Nothing that is borne for his sake, no matter how small, will lose its reward.

So, be ready for a fight if you wish to have victory. Without struggle and striving, you cannot win the reward of patience. If you refuse to suffer, you will be refused the crown. But if you desire to win the prize, strive bravely and endure patiently. Without effort or fighting, you cannot be victorious.

The Disciple

Please, O Lord by your grace, make what seems to be impossible—in light of human nature—be possible for me. You know how little I am able to bear and how quickly I become discouraged when adversity rises up against me. Whatever trial may come to me, may I view it as pleasing and acceptable, for to suffer and be tormented is exceedingly beneficial to my soul.

Book 3 Chapter 19

33

ON CHRIST'S OBEDIENCE TO THE FATHER

I have loved you even as the Father has loved me.
Remain in my love. When you obey my commandments,
you remain in my love, just as I obey
my Father's commandments and remain in his love.

John 15:9-10

The Christ

My friend, when you withdraw yourself from obedience, you also withdraw yourself from grace. And if you seek special privileges for yourself, you will lose privileges common to all. If you do not submit willingly to a superior but resist and complain, it is a sign that your human desires are not submissive to your own will. Learn quickly to submit yourself to those over you if you wish to bring yourself into subjection. If you have not conquered your inward enemies, the outward enemy can very quickly overcome you. And if you are not led by the Spirit, there is no more dangerous and deadly enemy to your soul than you are to yourself. You must have contempt for your sinful nature if you are to conquer your own flesh and blood. Because you are so in love with yourself, you shrink from yielding yourself to the will of others.

But what a great thing it is when you, who are dust and nothingness, yield yourself to other people for God's sake. Remember, I the Almighty and Most High, who created all things out of nothing, subjected myself to humanity for your sake. I became the most humble and despised human being so that my humility could overcome your pride. Learn to obey, O dust! Learn to humble yourself, O earth and clay, and bow beneath the feet of all. Learn to crush your passions and to yield yourself to all authority.

Be zealous to discipline yourself. Do not allow pride to live within you. So trample your pride under foot like dirt on the street. O foolish person, what do you have to complain about? O wicked sinner, what can you answer to those who speak against you since you have so often offended God and many times have deserved hell? But I have spared you, because your soul is precious in my sight. May you know my love and be thankful for my benefits. May you give yourself fully to true subjection and humility to patiently bear the contempt which you deserve.

Book 3 Chapter 13

34

ON THE FUTILE JUDGMENTS OF PEOPLE

It matters very little how I might be evaluated
by you or by any human authority.
I don't even trust my own judgment on this point.
My conscience is clear, but that doesn't prove I'm right.
It is the Lord himself who will examine me and decide.

1 Corinthians 4:3-4

The Christ

My friend, firmly anchor your soul upon God, and do not fear people's judgments when your conscience pronounces you righteous and innocent. It is good and blessed to suffer judgment, as it will not be painful to a heart that is humble and trusts God more than itself. Many people have many opinions, so don't put much trust in them. Besides, it is impossible to please all people. Even though, the apostle Paul wrote, "I try to find common ground with everyone" (1 Corinthians 9:22), he believed, "It matters very little how I might be evaluated by you or by any human authority. I don't even trust my own judgment on this point" (1 Corinthians 4:3).

Paul labored very hard, as much as he could, to bring salvation and encouragement to all people, but he could not avoid being judged and despised by others. So, he committed all to God, who knows all. By patience and humility, he defended himself against evil speakers, foolish and false thinkers, and those who accused him for their own pleasure. Nevertheless, from time to time, he defended himself for fear that his silence would become a stumbling block to those who were weak.

Who are you that you should be afraid of mortal humans? Today they are here, tomorrow they are gone! Fear God and you will not tremble at the terrors of his creation. What can a person do against you by words or deeds? Attackers will hurt themselves more than you and, whoever they may be, they will not escape the judgment of God. Keep your eyes on me and do not worry about cruel words. If now they cause pain and confusion that is not deserved, do not be impatient or allow it to diminish your reward. Instead, look up to me in heaven, for I am able to deliver you from all pain and confusion. I will reward all people for their works.

Book 3 Chapter 36

35

ON OBEDIENCE AND
SUBMISSION

---

*We know we love God's children if we love God
and obey his commandments.
Loving God means keeping his commandments,
and his commandments are not burdensome.*

1 John 5:2-3

The Disciple

It is a very great thing to live in obedience, to be under authority, and not to be independent. It is far safer to live under authority than be in a place of authority. Many people are in submission to authority out of fear rather than out of love. They miss the point and complain for little reason. They will not gain freedom of spirit unless, with all their hearts, they submit themselves to authority for the love of God. Though we run after peace, we will not find it until we humbly submit to those who are placed in authority over us. Daydreaming about a better situation has deceived many.

It's true that people willingly follow their own preferences and are more attracted to those who agree with them. But if Christ is among us, then it is necessary that we sometimes yield our own opinion for the sake of peace. No one is so wise as to have perfect knowledge of all things. So, let us not trust our own knowledge or opinions too much, but be willing to hear other people's perspective. Though our own opinions may be good, for the love of God and for the greater good, let them go and defer to the opinions of another.

I have often heard it is safer to listen and receive counsel than to give it. Yes, our opinions may be good, but to refuse to listen to others when the occasion requires it, is a mark of pride or stubbornness.

Book 1 Chapter 9

36

ON EARTHLY AFFECTIONS

For the Kingdom of God is not a matter of what
we eat or drink, but of living a life of goodness
and peace and joy in the Holy Spirit.
Romans 14:17

The Disciple

Whenever we desire success and prestige, we become restless. Proud and greedy people are never at peace, while the poor and humble of heart enjoy an abundance of peace. The person who is not completely dead to earthly affections is soon tempted and overcome by even small and trivial matters. It is hard for those who are weak in spirit and earthly-minded to overcome sensual desires. Therefore, when they are not indulging in worldly pleasures, they become sad and easily angered if anyone stands in the way of their desires.

Fortunately, when believers yield to these selfish inclinations, the Spirit immediately brings conviction to their conscience revealing that they have followed their own desires and not found the peace they had hoped to find. True peace of heart is found in resisting passions, not yielding to them.

Therefore, there is no peace in the heart of people who are earthly-minded. And neither is there peace for those who have simply given up earthly things to live a simple or stoic life. It is only Christ living in us, through his Spirit, that gives us peace.

Book 1 Chapter 6

37

ON THE MANY BENEFITS
OF OBEDIENCE

But don't just listen to God's word. You must do what it says.
Otherwise, you are only fooling yourselves. For if you listen to
the word and don't obey, it is like glancing at your face in
a mirror. You see yourself, walk away, and forget what you
look like. But if you look carefully into the perfect law that
sets you free, and if you do what it says and don't forget
what you heard, then God will bless you for doing it.

James 1:22-25

The Disciple

Open, O Lord, my heart to your law, and teach me to walk
in the way of your commandments. Grant me to understand
your will and be mindful of your benefits, both general and
specific, with great reverence and diligent meditation. May
I be able to worthily give you thanks. Yet I know and confess that I cannot offer you due praises for the least of your
mercies. I am less than the least of all the good things which

you have given me. When I consider your majesty, my spirit fails because of that great majesty.

All things which we have in the soul and in the body, and whatever things we possess, whether outwardly or inwardly, naturally or supernaturally are your good gifts. They prove that you, from whom we have received them all, are good, gentle, and kind. Although one person may receive many things and another fewer, yet all are yours, and without you not even the least thing can be possessed. People who have received greater blessings cannot boast that it is of their own merit nor lift themselves up above others nor show contempt to those beneath them. People who are holier and greater should consider themselves least and, in giving all thanks to God, should be more humble and devout. People who consider themselves less righteous and judge themselves to be unworthy of blessings are more likely to receive greater things.

But people who receive fewer gifts should not be discouraged, offended, or envious of those who are richer. They should look unto you and greatly praise your goodness, for you pour forth your gifts so richly, freely and largely, without respect of persons. All things come from you. So, in all things, you should be praised. You know what is best to give to each child and why this person has less and this person has more. It is not for us to understand because only you know how and why you distribute your blessings.

So, O Lord God, I consider it a great benefit to not have many things. That way my praise is not based on outward blessing, but only from my inward being. People who acknowledge their own poverty and sinfulness should not grieve, sorrow, or be sad in spirit. They will receive comfort and cheerfulness because you, Lord, have chosen the poor and humble of this world to be your friends. They have been made princes and princesses in all lands. In this world their lives were so humble and meek, without any malice or deceit, that they even rejoiced and "counted [themselves] worthy to suffer disgrace for the name of Jesus" (Acts 5:41). They embraced with great joy those things the world hated.

Therefore we ought to be contented and comforted, not by our outward blessings and benefits, but that God lifts up his peaceable and contented children in the lowest state to the highest place. And those of no fame or reputation, God considers more honorable and greater than others in the world. So, let us gain our honor and comfort in knowing we are loved by God.

Book 3 Chapter 22

38

ON SELF-DENIAL

"If you try to hang on to your life, you will lose it.
But if you give up your life for my sake, you will save it."
Matthew 16:25

The Christ

My friend, you cannot possess perfect freedom unless you completely deny yourself. Many are enslaved by riches, love for themselves, selfishness, curiosity, discontentedness, and by the search for creature comforts. These selfish things, which people continually plan, devise, and seek after are not my things and will pass away. Hold fast to this short but essential saying: "Give up all things and you will find all things; give up your lust and you will find rest." Meditate upon these truths, and when they fill your mind, you will understand all things.

This is not child's play or a fleeting hobby, but this is the pure goal of your faith.

My friend, you should not turn aside or be discouraged because you have heard the way is hard. Instead, you should strive toward a higher aim or at least desire to follow my perfect path. To do this, you must not love your own self, but always be listening to my guidance as your example. When you fully please me, you will go on in joy and peace. But you still have many selfish desires to reject if you want to find what you seek in me. "So I advise you to buy gold from me—gold that has been purified by fire. Then you will be rich" (Revelation 3:18). Heavenly wisdom despises all earthly rewards. So, put away all earthly wisdom and pleasure which is common to all people—and you!

I tell you, you must seek what is valuable in my sight, rather than the things considered great and valuable in the world. Do not seek to be honored on earth or to receive honor from human lips. Godly wisdom is a precious pearl which is hidden from many.

Book 3 Chapter 32

39

ON THE SURRENDER
OF SELF

My old self has been crucified with Christ.
It is no longer I who live, but Christ lives in me.
So I live in this earthly body by trusting in the Son of God,
who loved me and gave himself for me.

Galatians 2:20

The Christ

My friend, lose yourself and you will find me. Stand still with no thought of yourself, and you will receive great gain. For more grace will be given to you as you surrender yourself—as long as you do not turn back and put yourself first again.

The Disciple

O Lord, how often must I surrender myself, and in what things must I lose myself?

The Christ

In every hour and in every small and large way, there are no exceptions. You must surrender *everything* to me—every desire both outwardly and inwardly. And the more fully and sincerely you give me all things, the more abundantly you will be rewarded.

Some people surrender themselves with certain reservations, for they do not fully trust in God. They think they have to make provision for themselves. Other people, at first, offer me everything, but the pressure of temptation causes them to return to their own desires and plans. So, they make no progress in becoming like me. They will not gain the true freedom of a pure heart nor the grace of my sweet companionship. They must first entirely resign themselves and daily offer themselves up as a sacrifice. Without this, my union with them will not produce the fruit of righteousness.

Many times I have said to you and I now say it again: Give yourself up, surrender yourself, and you will have great inward peace. Give all for all. Demand nothing, ask nothing in return, but simply give with no reservations. Then you will possess me. You will have freedom of heart, and the darkness will not overcome you. Strive for this, pray for it, long after it, that you may be delivered from all selfish possessions and nakedly follow me, who was made naked for you. May you die to your own desires and live eternally to mine. Then all futile fantasies, evil confusion, overwhelming fears, unhealthy love, and unnecessary cares will die.

Book 3 Chapter 37

40

ON COMMITTING
OUR CAUSE TO CHRIST

Take delight in the LORD,
and he will give you your heart's desires.

Psalm 37:4

The Christ

My friend, always commit your cause to me. I will bring it to fulfillment at the right time. Wait for me to orchestrate all the details, and then you will be rewarded.

The Disciple

O Lord, freely and completely I commit all things to you, for my own planning gains me little. I wish I did not obsess on future events, but that I could offer myself completely to your pleasing will without delay.

The Christ

My friend, often people relentlessly strive after something they desire, but when they obtain it, they have already moved on to another goal. Their desires are not lasting, and they rush on from one thing to another. So it's not really a small thing when you surrender to me in small things.

The Disciple

True progress lies in self-denial, and people who deny themselves are free and safe. But our enemy, the opponent of all good things, never ceases from temptation, but day and night sets his traps so he can catch those who are unaware. "Keep watch and pray, so that you will not give in to temptation" (Matthew 26:41).

Book 3 Chapter 39

41

ON THE CHANGE
OF ONE'S WHOLE LIFE

Jesus replied, "'You must love the LORD your God
with all your heart, all your soul, and all your mind.'
This is the first and greatest commandment.
A second is equally important: 'Love your neighbor
as yourself.' The entire law and all the demands of
the prophets are based on these two commandments."

Matthew 22:37-40

The Disciple

We must be careful and diligent in God's service, and
always remember why we have rejected the world. Was
it not so we would live for God and become a spiritual
person? So, be passionate, as we will receive our heavenly
reward shortly. Within heaven's borders, there is neither
fear or sorrow. While we labor a little here, we will find
great rest and everlasting joy there. If we remain faithful
and enthusiastic in our work, we do not need to doubt that

THE IMITATION OF CHRIST

God will be faithful and generous in rewarding us. It is our duty to maintain hope that we will attain victory, but don't become over confident and fall into laziness and pride.

A certain man, having an anxious mind, was continually tossed between hope and fear. One day, being overwhelmed with grief, he slumped down in prayer before the church altar and thought to himself, *Oh, if I only knew if I will persevere.* He gently heard the voice of God within him saying, "And if you *did* know, what would you do? Do *now* what you would do then and you will be very secure." Immediately, he was comforted and strengthened, and the torment in his spirit disappeared. He committed himself to the will of God and no longer had any desire to know what he would face in the future. Instead, he began to study and seek the good, pleasing, and perfect will of God (Romans 12:2). The psalmist wrote, "Trust in the LORD and do good. Then you will live safely in the land and prosper" (Psalm 37:3). But there is often one thing holding us back from further progress and transformation: the dread of difficulty and conflict. But we can make great advancements in righteousness if we bravely strive to conquer those things which are most contrary and painful for us. Then, by overcoming our selfish spirit, more grace will be given us.

But we all have the same passions which must be conquered and killed. So whether we have strong passions or a calmer demeanor, we all must fervently pursue righteousness. Two things specifically give us the power to become more holy: a firm desire to withdraw ourselves from the sin to which we are most drawn and a passionate desire for the good that is most lacking. So, strive to earnestly guard against and subdue those faults that frequently harm others.

We must fill our minds with things that are beneficial to our souls, and whenever we see or hear good examples to imitate them. But whenever we see something that is not worthy, we must vow to not do it. And if we fail and do it, we must quickly repent of it. Just as our eyes look at others, remember the eyes of others are upon us. How sweet and pleasant it is to see passionate, godly people living out their faith and being examples of discipline. But how sad it is to see them walking in unrighteousness or not practicing their faith. How hurtful it is for people to neglect their godly calling and turn their attention to things which are none of their business.

We must be very aware of the duties we have undertaken and always look to the crucified Christ as our example and purposely conform our lives to his. Righteous people who are disciplined and devoutly committed to the holy and passionate life of our Lord will find all things necessary to spiritual growth abundantly provided in Jesus. If Jesus crucified and risen would come into our hearts, how quickly and completely would we learn all we need to know!

Fervent followers of Christ accept and bear well all things that are laid on them. But those who are careless and half-hearted experience trouble upon troubles. They suffer anguish on every side because they are without inward comfort. They are living under godly discipline and are exposed to terrible ruin. Those who seek easier and lighter discipline will always be in distress, because one thing or another gives them displeasure.

No assignment is given us except to praise the Lord our God with our whole heart and voice! We would be far happier if we never needed to eat, drink, sleep, or care for our many human needs. Then we could continuously praise God and give ourselves to spiritual exercises. If so, we would have never-ending spiritual refreshment, rather than the temporary blessings that we taste too seldom.

When people arrive at the point where they seek comfort from no created thing, they begin to perfectly enjoy God and are perfectly contented no matter what happens to them. They neither rejoice for much nor sorrow for little, because they fully commit themselves to trust God. In him, there is all fulfillment, where nothing perishes if we live in him and obey his every word without delay.

So let us always remember our end and how time that is lost is lost forever. Without care and diligence, we will never attain righteousness. If we begin to grow spiritually cold, it will not go well with us. But if we give ourselves to passionately pursuing God, we will find much peace. We will find our labor is lighter because of the grace of God and the love of virtue. People who are passionate and eager to serve God are ready for anything. It is harder work to resist sin and human passions than to do hard and physical labor. But if we do not shun small faults, we will surely fall little by little into greater sins. At evening, we will be glad if we spent the day profitably. We must watch over ourselves, stir ourselves up, warn ourselves not to worry what others do, and tend to our own soul. The harder we are on ourselves, the more we will benefit spiritually. Amen.

Book 1 Chapter 25

42

ON THE HOLY EXAMPLES
BEFORE US

---

*Therefore, since we are surrounded by such a huge crowd of
witnesses to the life of faith, let us strip off every weight that
slows us down, especially the sin that so easily trips us up.
And let us run with endurance the race God has set before us.*

Hebrews 12:1

The Disciple

Let us look to the vibrant examples of holy men and
women throughout history in whom shone the perfection
of Christ. Compared to them, we do little or nothing to
imitate Christ. They served our Lord in hunger and thirst,
while cold and poorly dressed, working until they were
exhausted, in spiritual disciplines and fasting, in prayer and
holy meditation, and in persecution and insults.

The apostles, church founders, those who suffered for
confessing their faith, those who died for not denying their
faith, and all those who walked in the footsteps of Christ all

loved their eternal souls more than they loved their physical lives. Some went so far as to live alone in the desert. But all suffered severe temptations and were attacked by the enemy. They offered frequent and fervent prayers unto God. They observed the discipline of fasting. With passionate zeal and strong desire for spiritual life, they offered themselves to God. They bravely disciplined themselves against sinful acts and thoughts so they could become masters over evil. Completely and faithfully, they sought after God! By day they labored in the world, and at night spent their time in prayer. Even as they went about their daily duties, they prayed mentally throughout the day.

They did not waste a minute of time, but spent every moment thinking of how they could use what they were currently doing to serve God. Sometimes they even forgot to eat and rest. They gave up all riches, dignities, honors, and friendships with the world. They desired nothing from the world, but only the bare necessities of life. Although, in appearance, they were poor in earthly things. They were rich above measure in grace, virtue, and heavenly blessings.

They were strangers to the world, but were welcomed as family and friends with God. In the world's eyes, they had no status or popularity, but in the sight of God they were precious and loved. They stood firm in true humility, lived in simple obedience, walked in love and patience, and so grew strong in spirit and obtained favor before God. They are given to us as an example. They should motivate us to live to please Christ and flee the lukewarm life of the world.

In the beginning, all those starting out on a spiritual journey are faithful in prayer, desirous of a holy life, and eager to follow a strict discipline of devotion. Unfortunately, many become careless in their travel and lose their fervency. They may stop altogether considering themselves reverent and holy simply because they are not sinning publicly.

We live in cold and complacent times, so that it is too easy to cool from fervent desire for Christ to casual luke-warmness. Wake up! Follow the example of godly witnesses who lived holy lives.

Book 18 Chapter 1

43

ON THE VALUE OF OURSELVES
IN THE SIGHT OF GOD

"It's all over! I am doomed, for I am a sinful man.
I have filthy lips, and I live among a people with filthy lips.
Yet I have seen the King, the LORD of Heaven's Armies."

Isaiah 6:5

The Disciple

I am only dust and ashes, but I will speak unto my Lord.
If I consider myself more than dust and ashes, I am lying
to myself and my sins testify to the truth. But if I am completely honest with myself, I realize that without God I have
no worth or value. "I was so foolish and ignorant—I must
have seemed like a senseless animal to you" (Psalm 73:22).

But God's grace favored me and enlightened my heart.
But if I think of my self-esteem rather than the esteem God
places on me, I will be swallowed up in my nothingness and
will perish forever. You, O God, show me the truth about
myself. Without you I am weak and nothing.

But when you look upon me, immediately I am made strong and filled with new joy. It is a great marvel that I am so suddenly lifted up so graciously by you, since I am always being pulled into the deep by my own weight.

This is the result of your love which so freely goes before me and nourishes me in so many ways. You guard me in great dangers and rescue me from innumerable evils. By loving myself—and not allowing you to love me—I nearly lost myself. But I now seek and sincerely love you alone. I found both myself *and* you. Through love, I have seen just how deep I fell. But you, O most sweet Lord, dealt with me beyond all that I deserved, above all I dared to ask or think.

Blessed be you, O my God, because though I was unworthy of all your benefits, your bountiful and infinite goodness never ceased to do good even to ungrateful creatures who have turned far from you. Turn us to yourself, that we may be grateful, humble, and godly, for you are our salvation, courage, and strength.

Book 3 Chapter 8

44

ON NOTHING WORTHY
OF OUR OWN GLORY

*This is a trustworthy saying, and everyone should accept it:
"Christ Jesus came into the world to save sinners"—and
I am the worst of them all. But God had mercy on me so that
Christ Jesus could use me as a prime example of his great
patience with even the worst sinners. Then others will realize
that they, too, can believe in him and receive eternal life.*

1 Timothy 1:15-16

The Disciple

"What are mere mortals that you should think about them,
human beings that you should care for them?" (Psalm 8:4).
What have people done to deserve your favor? Lord, how
can I complain if you forsake me? How can I justly accuse
you if you refuse to hear my prayers? Truthfully I can say,
Lord, without you I am nothing. I have nothing that is
good within myself. I fall short of your glory in all things.

Unless I am helped and inwardly supported by you, I become unfaithful and undisciplined.

But you, O Lord, are always the same and endure forever, always good, righteous, holy, doing all things well, and all wise. But I am more ready to go backward than forward. I am never satisfied and constantly wavering. Yet everything quickly becomes better when I please you and you put out your hand to help me. You alone can provide aid without the help of humans and can so strengthen me that my face always looks toward you. My heart is always turned to you, and I rest in you alone.

I wish I knew how to reject all human comforts, because no person can ever comfort me. I wish I would seek you more and become more devoted to you. Then I could worthily trust in your grace and rejoice in the gift of new comfort.

Thanks be to you, O God, from whom good things come! But I am useless and of no value in your sight, an ever-changing and weak human. What do I have in which to be proud or be held in honor? Is it all for nothing? This also is utterly vain. Yes, vain glory is an evil plague, the greatest of futility. It draws us away from the true glory and robs us of heavenly grace. While people please themselves, they displease you. While they lust for the praises of their peers, they deprive themselves of true virtues.

But true glory and holy joy comes not from glorifying ourselves, but in glorifying you; from not rejoicing in our own names, but rejoicing in yours. Let your work, not ours be magnified, O Lord. Let your holy name be blessed. But for me, let me not desire the praise of people. You are my glory. You are the joy of my heart. In you I will boast and be glad all day long, "I will boast only about my weaknesses" (2 Corinthians 12:5).

Let others seek honor that comes from one another, for they "gladly honor each other, but [they] don't care about the honor that comes from the one who alone is God" (John 5:44). When compared to your eternal glory, all human glory and earthly exaltation are truly futile and foolish. O God, my truth and my mercy, the blessed Trinity, to you alone "blessing and glory and wisdom and thanksgiving and honor and power and strength belong . . . forever and ever! Amen" (Revelation 7:12).

Book 3 Chapter 40

45

ON BEING A HUMBLE
IMITATOR OF CHRIST

For God called you to do good, even if it means suffering,
just as Christ suffered for you.
He is your example, and you must follow in his steps.

1 Peter 2:21

The Christ

I freely offered my will unto God the Father on the cross for your sins, with outstretched hands and naked body. Nothing remained in me that was not a sacrifice for divine judgment of sin. In the same way, every day you should offer yourself—with all your love and strength—to me as a pure and holy offering. I only require that you completely offer yourself to me. I do not desire anything from you—other than yourself. I don't ask for your gifts, only you.

It would be insufficient for you to have all things on earth but not me. In the same way, it would be insufficient if you gave me everything except yourself. Offer yourself to me. Give yourself completely to God so that your offering will be accepted. Remember, I offered myself completely to the Father for you. I also gave my whole body and blood for your nourishment so that you are mine and I am yours. But if you depend on yourself, and don't offer yourself freely to my will, your offering is not perfect. The union between us will be incomplete.

If you wish to attain liberty and grace, then freely offer yourself into the hands of God before you offer your works. For this is the reason, so few are inwardly enlightened and made free; they do not entirely deny themselves. My word stands sure: "You cannot become my disciple without giving up everything you own" (Luke 14:33). So, if you wish to be my disciple, offer yourself to me completely with all your heart.

Book 4 Chapter 8

46

ON THE GUARD OF HUMILITY

And all of you, dress yourselves in humility as you relate to one another, for "God opposes the proud but gives grace to the humble." So humble yourselves under the mighty power of God, and at the right time he will lift you up in honor.

1 Peter 5:5b-6

The Christ

My friend, it is better and safer to keep your devotional life hidden and not boast about it. Do not to speak much about yourself nor have pride in your devotions. Rather humble yourself, and realize that you are unworthy of grace. And do not depend too much on spiritual emotions, for they can quickly turn to the opposite feeling. When you are sensing abundant grace, think about how miserable and poor you would be without it.

And if you desire to keep advancing in your spiritual life, don't neglect prayer if the sense of grace is taken from you. React to this humbly and patiently, and maintain your spiritual exercises so you will gain more strength and knowledge during this time. Do not neglect yourself because of this barren time with its anxiety of spirit. "I know, LORD, that our lives are not our own. We are not able to plan our own course" (Jeremiah 10:23). It is God's privilege to give and comfort whom he wishes, when he wishes, and as much as he wishes. Some who become presumptuous because of the grace poured out on them have destroyed themselves. They tried to do more than they were able. They did not consider how weak they really were. They followed the impulses of their heart rather than the judgment of reason. And because they presumed to do more than was pleasing to God, they quickly lost his favor. They became poor and sinful for they tried to build a nest in the heavens. They were humbled and brought back to earth with poverty, so they might learn not to fly with their own wings, but put their trust in his feathers. Those who are young and not wise in the way of the Lord, must place themselves under the counsel of the wise; otherwise they will be easily deceived and led astray.

But if they wish to follow their own fantasies, rather than trust the experience of others, the result will be very dangerous to them. They must not depend on their own ideas. Those who are wise in their own eyes, seldom submit to the authority of others. It is better to have a small amount of wisdom and little understanding with humility, than great human knowledge with vain self-esteem. It is better for you to have less than much of what may make you proud. People who give up themselves for earthly pleasure are not wise. They have forgotten their former helplessness, the pure reverence of the Lord, and fear of losing my grace offered. Nor are people very wise, who in times of adversity or any kind of trouble, despair and do not trust me fully as they should.

People who seek security in earthly peace instead will be in despair and full of fear. But if you learn humbly with self-control, if you rule and guide your own spirit well, you would not so quickly fall into danger and disgrace. When the flames of devotion are within your soul, it is wise to consider how it will be with you when the light is taken away. And when the light is extinguished, remember that eventually the light will return. I have taken away the light as a warning so you will trust in *me* and not the light. Such a trial is often more useful than if you had lived a prosperous life by your own efforts.

Do not consider people great who have had many visions and blessing, are skilled in the Scriptures, or placed in high positions. God considers you great if you are grounded upon true humility, are filled with divine love, always sincerely seek to honor God with an upright life, have not isolated yourself from others, and have rejoiced to be despised and humbled by others rather than to be honored.

Book 3 Chapter 7

47

ON THINKING HUMBLY
OF ONESELF

Don't think you are better than you really are.
Be honest in your evaluation of yourselves,
measuring yourselves by the faith God has given us.

Romans 12:3

The Disciple

Every person has a natural desire to gain knowledge, but what is the benefit of knowledge without the reverence of God? Lowly peasants, who serve God, have a greater reward than conceited intellectuals, who set their sights on higher learning but neglect to know themselves.

People who know themselves know their shortcomings and don't take the praises of others seriously. If I knew all the knowledge of the entire world and was not living in love, how would that help me before God who will judge me according to my deeds (1 Corinthians 13:1-3)?

We should not wear ourselves out with an unhealthy desire for knowledge, for we will find ourselves distracted and deceived. We may seek knowledge, appear learned, and be called wise, but there is much we can learn that does not benefit our soul in any way. And if we study hard those things that do not contribute to the health of our soul, we are immeasurably foolish. Many wise words do not satisfy the soul, but a righteous life refreshes the mind, and a clear conscience assures great confidence before God.

The greater and more advanced our knowledge, the more severely we will be judged—unless we live a holy life. So, let us not exalt ourselves with the skills and knowledge we can acquire, but guard the holy knowledge we have been given. If it seems we know many things and understand them well, know also there are many other things which we do not know. We must not be high-minded but confess our ignorance. Why do we want to lift ourselves above another person, when we may learn that they are more knowledgeable and understanding of Scripture than we are? To know and learn anything that is helpful, be content to be unknown and not respected.

The highest and most beneficial lesson is to consider others wiser and more knowledgeable than we are. To think less of ourselves and more highly and kindly of others is the way to be truly great and wise. Even if we see our neighbors sin openly and shamefully, we shouldn't consider ourselves better than them, because we don't know how long we can maintain our own integrity. All of us are weak and frail, so don't consider anyone less spiritual than yourself.

Book 1 Chapter 2

48

ON LOWLY SUBMISSION

"The greatest among you must be a servant.
But those who exalt themselves will be humbled,
and those who humble themselves will be exalted."
Matthew 23:11-12

The Disciple

We must not be greatly concerned with who is for us or against us, but concentrate on our present responsibilities. Let us take care that God is with us in whatever we do. If we keep a clear conscience, God will defend us. No person's perverse attacks will be able to hurt us. If we know how to keep our peace when we suffer offenses, we will no doubt see the help of the Lord. He knows when and how to deliver us, so we must submit ourselves totally to God. He is the one who will help us and deliver us from all conflicts. Often God allows others to know our faults and to rebuke us for them. This makes us more humble.

When people acknowledge their own defects, they can live in peace with others and quickly pacify those who are against them. God protects and delivers humble people. He loves and comforts them. He draws close to the humble and pours out great grace upon them. And when they are beaten down, he raises them to glory. He reveals his secrets to the humble and draws close to them. He invites them into his presence. When humble people are criticized, they remain at peace because they depend on God and not the world. We can consider ourselves blessed if we don't feel superior to anyone.

Book 2 Chapter 2

49

ON HUMBLE WORKS

If you are wise and understand God's ways,
prove it by living an honorable life, doing good works
with the humility that comes from wisdom.

James 3:13

The Christ

My friend, you are not always able to wholeheartedly seek my virtues or to keep your mind on heavenly things. Sometimes, because of your human nature, you become weary and unwillingly fall to worldly desires and bear the consequences of this corruptible life. So long as you live in this body, you will become weary and will have a heavy heart. So, you ought to grieve the burden of living in this earthly body, because you cannot give yourself fully to spiritual studies and to increasing the divine meditation you desire.

At such times, it's important to turn to humble and manual labor to renew yourself with good deeds. Wait with confidence for my heavenly presence. Bear this mental and spiritual bareness with patience until you sense my presence again, and you will be freed from all anxieties. I will cause you to forget your spiritual weariness and to discover my peace. I will open up pleasant passages of Scripture that will encourage your heart so you my run according to my commandments. And you will say, "What we suffer now is nothing compared to the glory he will reveal to us later" (Romans 8:18).

Book 3 Chapter 51

50

ON CONTEMPT OF
ALL TEMPORAL HONOR

Human pride will be brought down,
and human arrogance will be humbled.
Only the LORD will be exalted on that day of judgment.

Isaiah 2:11

The Christ

My friend, don't spend time worrying if you see others honored and praised, while you are despised and humbled. Lift up your thoughts to me in heaven, then the contempt of people on earth won't make you sad.

The Disciple

O Lord, we are so blind to what is really important and are quickly seduced by earthly, meaningless things. If I'm honest with myself, I have nothing to complain about since no human has fatally injured me. But there have been many times when I have seriously sinned against you, so all your creations could justly condemn me. I deserve only shame and contempt, but you have showered upon me praise, honor, and glory. I must accept that all humans who are not spiritually enlightened will despise me, desert me, and consider me nothing, but when I am united with you, I am filled with peace and strength.

Book 3 Chapter 41

51

ON CONTEMPT OF VAIN AND WORLDLY KNOWLEDGE

Remember, dear brothers and sisters, that few of you
were wise in the world's eyes or powerful or
wealthy when God called you. Instead, God
chose things the world considers foolish in order
to shame those who think they are wise.
And he chose things that are powerless
to shame those who are powerful.

1 Corinthians 1:26-27

The Christ

My friend, do not let beautiful and sweet sounding compliments affect you. "For the Kingdom of God is not just a lot of talk; it is living by God's power" (1 Corinthians 4:20). Listen to my words, for they will inspire your heart and enlighten your mind. They bring repentance and provide abundant comfort. Never read the Word so you may appear learned or wise, but study it to overcome your sins. This will be far more profitable for you than being able to answer many difficult questions.

When you have read and studied many things, you must always return to the one first principle: I know everything (Psalm 94:10). I give children clearer knowledge than can be taught by adults. The one to whom I speak will quickly become wise and will grow abundantly in the Spirit. But woe to those who inquire into the curious questions of their peers and take little heed to the ways of my service. The time will come when I will appear—the Teacher of teachers and the Lord of the angels—and I will examine the wisdom and thoughts of each one. "I will search with lanterns in Jerusalem's darkest corners" (Zephaniah 1:12). I "will bring [your] darkest secrets to light and will reveal [your] private motives" (1 Corinthians 4:5). Then all arguments of human tongues will be silenced.

I am the One, who in an instant lifts up humble spirits so they can learn greater wisdom of eternal truth than the person who studied ten years in schools. I teach without the noise of words, without confusion of opinions, without striving after honors, without the clash of arguments. I am the One who teaches my friends to despise earthly things; to loath present, temporary things; to seek after heavenly things; to enjoy eternal delights; to flee honors; to endure all offenses; to place all hope in me; to desire nothing apart from me; and above all earthly things, to love only me.

For there are people, who by loving me from the bottom of their hearts, learn divine truth and speak wonderful wisdom. They gain more by forsaking all earthly things than by studying theological subtleties. To some I speak common truth, while to others deeper wisdom. To some, I appear gentle and soft-spoken, while to others I reveal mysteries with blinding light. The Word of God is one, but it doesn't inform all alike. Inwardly, I am the Teacher of truth, the Searcher of the heart, the Discerner of all thoughts, the Mover of all actions, distributing them to each person as I judge best.

Book 3 Chapter 43

52

ON THE GRACE OF GOD

*"And now I entrust you to God and the message of
his grace that is able to build you up and give you
an inheritance with all those he has set apart for himself."*

Acts 20:32

The Disciple

Why do we seek rest, when we were born to work? Let us
prepare ourselves more for patience rather than for comfort; for bearing the cross than for joy. For who among the
people of earth would not rather gladly receive comfort
and spiritual joy if they could have it? For spiritual comfort
exceeds all the delights of this world and all the pleasures
of the body. For all worldly delights apart from Christ are
either empty or unclean. But only spiritual delights are
pleasant and honorable, the result of virtue and poured
forth by God into pure minds. But we cannot continually
enjoy these divine comforts by our own efforts, because
temptation will not cease for long.

There is a great difference between a visitation from above and the false spirit of confidence in oneself. God does well in giving us the grace of comfort, but people don't do well in immediately giving him thanks for it. As a result, the gift of grace is not able to flow into us, because we are ungrateful to the Source of it. We must return it to the fountain from which it flows. For grace always fills people who are humbly grateful for it, and is taken away from the proud people who are lacking humility.

I do not desire any comfort which takes me away from the knowledge of my spiritual emptiness. I do not love any thoughts which lead me to pride. For what the world honors highly is not holy, nor is everything that tastes sweet good. Every desire is not pure, nor is everything dear to us pleasing to God. Willingly, I accept the grace which makes me more humble, more wary of worldly things, and more willing to give up my rights. People who gain knowledge by the gift of grace and are taught wisdom by being humbled will not dare to claim any good thing for themselves. Rather, they will confess that they are poor and needy. "Give to God what belongs to God" (Matthew 22:21). Do not consider those things as belonging to you, but give thanks to God for grace. We must confess our faults and realize we deserve punishment for those faults. At a banquet, "take the lowest place at the foot of the table. Then when your host sees you, he will come and say, 'Friend, we have a better place for you!' Then you will be honored in front of all the other guests" (Luke 14:10). For we cannot be the highest in the kingdom without being the lowest here on earth. For the highest saints of God are the least in their own sight, and the more glorious they are, the lower they consider themselves. They are full of grace and heavenly glory, but do not desire earthly glory. They rest on God and the strength of his might. They cannot be lifted up any other way. And the people who give God credit for all the good they have received, seek glory not from each other, but "care about the honor that comes from the one who alone is God" (John 5:44). All God's saints are always striving for this very thing: that God should be praised for his own glorious self.

So as a result, when we are thankful for the smallest of benefits, we will receive ever greater ones. Let the least blessing be considered the greatest and those things considered the least be viewed as a special gift from God. For if we consider the majesty of the Giver, nothing given by him should be considered nothing, small, or of no worth. For what gift can be considered small if given by the Most High God? Even if he gives us punishments and injuries, we ought to be thankful, because he doesn't do it to make us suffer but to make us like his Son (Romans 8:29). If we want to retain God's favor, we must be thankful for the favor he has given us and be patient when favor is taken away. Pray that it may return, but first be cautious and humble that we do not lose it.

Book 2 Chapter 10

53

ON THE VALUE OF
DIVINE GRACE

*So to keep me from becoming proud, I was given
a thorn in my flesh, a messenger from Satan to torment me
and keep me from becoming proud. Three different times
I begged the Lord to take it away. Each time he said,
"My grace is all you need. My power works best in weakness."*

2 Corinthians 12:7-9

The Disciple

O Lord, my God, you have created me in your own image and likeness. Please grant me this: after you have done so great and necessary work of salvation, may I conquer my wicked nature which draws me to sin and unrighteousness. For I feel in my body the law of sin, which contradicts the law of my mind. This makes me captive and coerced by my sensual desires. I cannot resist its passion unless your most fervent, holy grace assists me and is poured into my heart.

Yes, if my nature is to be conquered, I need your grace in abundant measure. It has always been prone to evil from my youth. For, because of the fall of the first man, Adam, I am corrupted by sin and the punishment of this stain has been passed on to all people. All nature, which was created good and righteous by you, is now corrupted and spreads sin and unrighteousness. It draws all people to evil and base desires. For there is little power for good except one spark buried among the ashes. Nature's wisdom is wrapped with thick clouds. Yet there is discernment of good and evil, a distinction between truth and falsehood. But it is powerless in its own power to fulfill all it approves of. There is not the full light of truth or healthiness in its wants and desires.

So, O my God, I take delight in your law. For "still, the law itself is holy, and its commands are holy and right and good. . . . I love God's law with all my heart" (Romans 7:12, 22). Yet, I know in my body, I serve the law of sin, and I obey sensuality rather than reason. "I know that nothing good lives in me, that is, in my sinful nature. I want to do what is right, but I can't" (Romans 7:18).

I often purpose to do many good things, but because grace is lacking in my weaknesses, I fall back with little resistance and fail. Because of this, I recognize the way of perfection and see clearly what I should do. But pressed down by the weight of my own corruption, I don't rise to the things which are perfect.

Your grace is entirely necessary, O Lord, for a good beginning, good progress, and a good completion of life. Without your grace, I can do nothing, but "I can do everything through [you], who gives me strength" (Philippians 4:13). We are powerless, for without your heavenly grace, no gift of nature has any value. Arts, riches, beauty, strength, wit, or eloquence cannot do anything without you, O Lord, and your grace.

For the gifts of nature are both good and evil alike. But your gifts of loving grace bear the mark of everlasting life. This grace is so mighty, that without it, the gifts of prophecy, the working of miracles, or any wisdom—no matter how lofty—have any value at all. Likewise, faith and hope, nor any other virtue is acceptable to God without love and grace (1 Corinthians 13:2).

Grace makes the poor in spirit rich in righteousness. It makes the rich in many ways humble in spirit. Fill me with your comfort so that my soul does not fail through weariness and drought of mind. I plead with you, O Lord, may I find grace in your sight when I have earthly needs, for only your grace is sufficient for me (2 Corinthians 12:9). When I am tempted and tormented by many troubles and trials, I will fear no evil as long as your grace remains with me.

Your grace is alone my strength, for it brings me counsel and help. It is more powerful than all my enemies and wiser than all the wise ones in the world.

Grace is the mistress of truth, the teacher of discipline, the light of the heart, the comfort in anxiety, the reliever of sorrow, the deliverer from fear, the nurse of devotion, and the source of tears of joy. I am just a withered tree without it, a dried-out branch to be cast away. Let your grace, then, always protect and be with me. May it prompt me to continually give good works through Jesus Christ, your Son. Amen.

Book 3 Chapter 55

54

ON THE GRACE
OF DEVOTION

*God's law was given so that all people could see
how sinful they were. But as people sinned more and more,
God's wonderful grace became more abundant.
So just as sin ruled over all people and
brought them to death, now God's wonderful grace
rules instead, giving us right standing with God
and resulting in eternal life through
Jesus Christ our Lord.*

Romans 5:20-21

The Christ

Earnestly seek the grace of devotion. Wait patiently and
faithfully for it, so you may receive it gratefully, preserve
it humbly, work with it diligently, and allow God to determine when your awareness of it may come. Most of all,
humble yourself when you feel little or no devotion. Do
not be discouraged or grieve the lack of feelings. Often God

pours out, in one short moment, all that he has withheld from you for so long. He often gives grace, which he has so long delayed, at the end of a lengthy time of prayer.

The Disciple

If grace was always given immediately—whenever we wished—it would be hard for us, as weak humans, to bear. So, wait for grace with good hope and humble patience. Blame it on yourself and your sins when it is not given or mysteriously taken away. Sometimes, it's a small thing that hinders or hides grace. (Sometimes what we may think is a "small" thing may be very great in God's eyes.) But if we will remove this small or great impediment and perfectly overcome it, we will have the grace we asked for.

We must completely offer ourselves to God with all our heart, not wanting our own desires or pleasures, but trusting him for everything. Then we will find ourselves whole and at peace. Nothing gives us such sweet joy and delight as the good, pleasing, and perfect will of God (Romans 12:2). People, who lift up their will to God with pure motives and give themselves to holy love and hatred for created things, are the most fit and worthy for receiving grace and the gift of devotion. For wherever the Lord finds empty vessels, he pours out his blessings (2 Kings 4:1-7). The more you forsake things that have no heavenly value and die to your own desires, the more abundantly grace floods in and the higher it lifts your free heart.

"Your eyes will shine, and your heart will thrill with joy, for merchants from around the world will come to you. They will bring you the wealth of many lands" (Isaiah 60:5), for the hand of the Lord is with you. If we place ourselves wholly in his hand forever, we will be blessed. We will be blessed if we seek God with all our hearts. When we take Holy Communion, we receive the great grace of divine union. We do not think of our own devotion and comfort, but we meditate on Christ's devotion and comfort, to the glory and honor of God.

Book 4 Chapter 15

55

ON THE CONFIDENCE
OF GRACE

*Whatever is good and perfect is a gift coming down
to us from God our Father, who created all the lights
in the heavens. He never changes or casts a shifting shadow.*

James 1:17

The Christ

My friend, I am good and "a strong refuge when trouble
comes" (Nahum 1:7). Come to me whenever it is not well
with you.

When you are too slow to call to me in prayer, this
causes a lack in heavenly comfort. Before you earnestly seek
me, you first seek after many other means of comfort. You
refresh yourself with outward things. So you find that all
these earthly things have not helped you at all. You must
learn that I am the only one you can trust to deliver you.
There is no strong help, no helpful counsel, or no lasting
remedy but me. But now, as you recover courage following

your storm, grow strong in the light of my mercies. For, I the Lord, say that I restore all things, not only as they were at the beginning, but more abundantly and stacked higher than they once were.

"I am the LORD, the God of all the peoples of the world. Is anything too hard for me?" (Jeremiah 32:27). Where is your faith? Stand firm with perseverance. Be patient and strong. Comfort will come to you at the right time. Wait for me. Yes, wait. I will come and heal you. When temptation troubles you and unfounded fears terrify you, remember this: "Don't worry about tomorrow, for tomorrow will bring its own worries. Today's trouble is enough for today" (Matthew 6:34). It is futile and useless to be disturbed or wrought up about future things which may never come.

But it is human nature to be deceived by these fallacies. It is a sign that your mind is still weak as it is so easily distracted at the threat of an enemy. For the enemy does not care if he can deceive you with something that is true or false, whether it is the love of the present or fear of the future. "I am leaving you with a gift—peace of mind and heart. And the peace I give is a gift the world cannot give. So don't be troubled or afraid" (John 14:27). When you think you are far removed from me, I am often the closest. When you determine almost all is lost, then there is often a greater opportunity at hand. All is not lost when something goes contrary to your wishes. Do not judge something according to your present feelings or grieve any time something goes wrong. Do not believe there is no hope of escape.

Do not think of yourself as being totally abandoned, even though I have sent to you some trials and troubles and even withdrawn some cherished comforts. No, this is the way to the kingdom of heaven. Without a doubt, it is better for you—and for all of my other servants—that you should be proven by adversities rather than having everything the way you would like it. I know your hidden thoughts. It is very necessary for your soul's health that you should sometimes be left without joy, so you won't be lifted up by prosperity and won't desire to please only yourself. What I have given, I am able to take away—and then restore again—all for my good pleasure.

What I have given is mine. When I take it away, I have not taken what is yours. "Whatever is good and perfect [comes] down to us from God our Father" (James 1:17). These good things come through me. When you experience grief or frustration, do not be angry, and do not let your heart be sad. I am able to quickly lift you up and change every burden into joy. I am just and greatly to be praised when I do these things to you.

If you will look at this, the right way with truth, you will never be so discouraged by adversity, but will rejoice and give thanks. Yes, consider it the highest honor that I do not spare you from sorrows. As I have spoken to my beloved disciples, "I have loved you even as the Father has loved me" (John 15:9). I sent them, not unto worldly joys, but to great conflicts; not unto honors, but contempt; not unto ease, but to hard labors; not unto rest, but to bring much fruit through patience. My friend, remember these words.

Book 3 Chapter 30

56

ON BEARING WITH
THE FAULTS OF OTHERS

Forgive us our sins,
as we forgive those who sin against us.
And don't let us yield to temptation.

Luke 11:4

The Disciple

Those things we cannot change in ourselves, we ought
to patiently bear until God intervenes. Often it's better
to bear trials and be patient than to try to change them.
Nevertheless, when we learn of our own shortcomings, we
ask God to give us strength to bear with goodwill that same
flaw in others.

If someone is warned once or twice but refuses to listen,
don't struggle with him or her, but commit them and the
situation to God. Pray that his will may be done and his
honor shown in all his children, because he knows how to
transform evil into good. Let us be patient in bearing with

others' faults and weakness—whatever they be—because we ourselves have many things which others must bear.

If we can't make our own selves into the people we desire to be, how will we be able to change someone into our own liking? We are anxious to see others made perfect, and yet we don't change our own shortcomings!

We want others immediately corrected, but we won't correct ourselves. The freedom of others displeases us, but we are in no hurry to correct our own faults. We want rules that restrain others, but we will not tolerate our own wishes being restrained. So, it plainly appears that we seldom weigh ourselves on the same balance as we weigh our neighbors. If every person was perfect, we wouldn't have to be patient with other people.

But God has commanded that we learn to bear one another's burdens, because none of us is without defect, none without a burden, none self-sufficient, none wise enough. But it is the responsibility of each person to bear one another's shortcomings, to comfort one another, to help, to instruct, and to warn one another. How much strength we have is best proven by how we handle adversity. Such occasions do not make us weak, but show our strength.

Book 1 Chapter 16

57

ON EVIL WORDS CAST UPON US

"God blesses you when people mock you and persecute you
and lie about you and say all sorts of evil things against you
because you are my followers. Be happy about it!
Be very glad! For a great reward awaits you in heaven."
Matthew 5:11-12

The Christ

My friend, stand firm and trust in me. For what are words
but only words? They fly through the air, but they do no
harm. If you are guilty, think of ways that you can change.
If you know there is nothing against you, then bear this
gladly for God's sake. If you can't bear to hear gentle correction now, when will you be able to bear harsh criticism?
And why do such trivial words pierce your heart? Because
you are still earthly minded and regard people's words more
than you should. If you fear criticism, it is because you are
unwilling to be corrected for your faults and would rather
make excuses.

But look closer into yourself and you will see that the world's values and the futile hope of pleasing people are still alive inside you. For when you flee from being corrected and confronted for your faults, it is plain that you are neither humble nor truly dead to the world's values. The world is not crucified in you. But listen to my word, and you will not care about ten thousand of the world's words. Even if someone told the most perverse lies about you, what would it hurt you if you let it go and paid little attention to it? Could it harm a hair on your head?

But people, who have no love for me within themselves and do not have God before their eyes, are easily upset by a word of criticism. But people who trust in me and do not live by their own judgments will be free from the fear of people's judgments. I am the judge and discerner of all secrets. I know the complete story: both the criticizer and the criticized. I allowed those words to be spoken; by my permissions they were spoken. "As a result, the deepest thoughts of many hearts will be revealed" (Luke 2:35).

The testimony of people is often deceptive, but my judgment is true. It will stand and will not be overturned. Often my judgments are not seen, for only in rare cases are they made known. But my judgments are never in error, although they may not seem right to the eyes of people who do not believe in God. To me, therefore, must all people submit to my judgments and not depend on their own opinions. "No harm comes to the godly, but the wicked have their fill of trouble" (Proverbs 12:21).

Even if some unjust charge is brought against you, you should care little. And even if you are praised above measure, you are not completely proven correct. For I "look deep within the mind and heart" (Psalm 7:9).

The Disciple

O Lord God, my Judge, you are just, strong, and patient. You know the weakness and sinfulness of people. Be my strength and my total confidence. My own conscience is not sufficient. You know what I do not know, and therefore under criticism I should humble myself and bear it meekly. So, please mercifully forgive me, as I have often not done this. And next time, grant me the grace to endure greater criticism. Your abundant grace and mercy is better for me. "My conscience is clear, but that doesn't prove I'm right. It is [you] who will examine me and decide" (1 Corinthians 4:4). If your mercy was removed, I would not be justified. "For you are God, my only safe haven" (Psalm 43:2).

Book 3 Chapter 46

58

ON THE INWARD GROWTH OF PATIENCE

We . . . pray that you will be strengthened with
all his glorious power so you will have all the endurance
and patience you need. May you be filled with joy.

Colossians 1:11

The Disciple

O Lord God, I see that patience is so very necessary for me, for many things in this life work against me. For as much as I work for peace, my life cannot go on without strife or trouble.

The Christ

You speak the truth, my friend. For my desire is that you don't define peace as life without trials and adversities. Rather, you should consider yourself to have found peace when you are tested with many trials and proven by many troubles. If you say you cannot bear much now, how will you survive greater trials? When faced with two evils, you should always choose the least. Therefore if you are to survive future trials, strive with God's strength to bear the present evils bravely. Do you think that the children of this world suffer little or nothing? Even the most prosperous people face suffering.

But you will say, "Those who do not obey God have many worldly pleasures. They follow their own wills and bear few trials and troubles."

Granted, they enjoy what you list, but how long do you think it will last? Like smoke, those who are rich in this world will pass away and their joys will be gone. Even while they are alive, their rest is disturbed with bitterness, weariness, and fear. For from the very same things in which they find delight, they often suffer the punishment of sorrows. Consequently, because they are seeking and pursuing pleasure, they don't enjoy them but suffer confusion and bitterness. Oh how short, how false, how excessive, and how wicked are these pleasures! Because of their drunkenness and moral blindness, they "are like unthinking animals, creatures of instinct, born to be caught and destroyed. They scoff at things they do not understand, and like animals, they will be destroyed" (2 Peter 2:12). But "take delight in the LORD, and he will give you your heart's desires" (Psalm 37:4).

If you are to truly find joy and be abundantly comforted by me, you must have contempt for all worldly things and worthless pleasures. Then blessings and complete comfort will be given to you. And the more you withdraw yourself from the pleasure of creature comforts, the sweeter and more powerful comfort you will find in me. But it will take repentance and hard work to attain these comforts. You will need to oppose deeply ingrained habits, but you will overcome with better habits. Your body will groan again and again, but you will be restrained by the power of my Spirit. The old enemy will tempt you and make you bitter, but he will be put to flight by prayer. By meaningful labor, you will block the enemy from entering your life.

Book 3 Chapter 12

59

ON PATIENCE WITH OURSELVES

Be patient with everyone.

1 Thessalonians 5:14

The Christ

My friend, your patience and humility during adversities are more pleasing to me than your devotion in prosperity. Why do little things spoken against you make you sad? You should not have been affected even if the adversity had been stronger. Now allow the offence to pass. It is not the first offence, and it will not be the last if you live a long life. You are brave enough when you meet no opposition. You give good counsel. You know how to strengthen others with your words. But when troubles and trials suddenly show up at your own door, your own counsel and strength fail. Consider your great weakness when faced with trifling matters. These things come so that your soul will be made stronger.

Put these struggles out of your mind as well as you can. And if troubles have struck you, don't let it discourage or trip you up you for very long. At the least bear it patiently if you cannot bear it joyfully. And although you may feel resentment toward the trial, check yourself and don't allow any reactionary words to come from your mouth that may offend younger believers. Soon the storm which has risen against you will be stilled and inward grief will be comforted by returning grace. I, the Lord, say I live to help you and will give you your desired comfort if you put your trust in me and call sincerely to me.

Remain calm in your spirit, and prepare yourself for greater endurance. Nothing is out of control—even though you find yourself attacked and seriously tempted. You are a human being and not God; you are flesh and not an angel. So, how could you always remain in a state of righteousness when angels in heaven and the first couple fell? I am the One who lifts up mourners and those who know their own weaknesses to deliverance. I raise you up to my own nature.

The Disciple

O Lord, your words are a blessing, sweeter than honey from the honeycomb. What could I do in my great troubles and anxieties unless you comforted me with your holy words?

If I am safe in the haven of your salvation, what does it matter if I suffer? Grant me a good end to my life and a happy passage from this world. Remember me, O my God, and lead me on the right path to your kingdom. Amen.

Book 3 Chapter 57

60

ON THE LOVE OF
SOLITUDE AND SILENCE

Be still in the presence of the LORD,
and wait patiently for him to act.

Psalm 37:7

The Disciple

Let us find a suitable time for our meditation and think frequently about the mercies of God to us. We must ignore questions that merely stimulate our curiosity. Study writings that cause you to sorrow for your sins rather than simply amuse you. If we withdraw from trivial conversations and idle goings on, novel ideas and gossip, we will find sufficient time for helpful meditation. The greatest saints used to avoid the company of people and chose to live isolated lives with God. One saint said, "As often as I've been among people, I have often returned less a person." We often experience this when we have spent a long time in conversation. It is easier to remain silent than to say too much. It is easier

176

to stay home alone than to sufficiently guard yourself when you are out in a crowd. If you wish to obtain what is hidden and spiritual, you must go to Jesus and not to people.

We cannot go safely abroad if we do not love the solitude of home. We cannot safely talk unless we love to hold our peace. We cannot safely supervise unless we love to be subject to other people. We cannot safely make rules unless we love to obey. We cannot safely rejoice unless we have a clear conscience within us.

The boldness of the saints was always prompted by the fear of God. They were diligent and humbled themselves, yet demonstrated great virtues and grace. But the boldness of wicked people springs from pride and a high opinion of themselves, but in the end turns to their own confusion. Never promise yourself security in this life, even if you are a devout follower of Christ.

Often those who receive the highest praise of people, fall more seriously because of their great self-confidence. It is very beneficial if we face inward temptation and are frequently assaulted, so that we will not become overly confident, lifted up by pride, or dependent on the comforts of this world. How clear a conscience we will have if we never seek temporary joy that passes away and never become entangled in the world. What a great peace and calm we will possess if we throw away useless things and think only of healthful and divine things. Let us build our hope solely upon God!

We are not worthy of heavenly comforts unless we have diligently disciplined ourselves with holy restraint. If we feel any anxiety within our hearts, let us find a quiet place and shut out the commotion of the world. As it is written, "Think about it overnight and remain silent" (Psalm 4:4). In quiet evenings at home, we will often find what we have lost outside during the day. If we continue in this quiet time, we will find sweet rest. But if we don't, we will become weary. If we will keep our quiet time well, it will become a dear friend and a most pleasant retreat. In silence, the devout follower of Christ makes progress and learns the hidden things of the Scriptures. There we will find a fountain of tears with which to wash and purify ourselves each night so we may grow closer to our Maker and move farther away from all worldly distractions. If we withdraw ourselves from our friends and acquaintances, God will come close with his angels. It is better to be unknown and know ourselves than work miracles and not know our spiritual condition. If we are to receive praise from God, we must not go out into the world to simply see and be seen by others.

Why would we want to see things to which God has said no? The world and its lusts pass away. Sensual desires draw us into the world, but in the end, what do we bring home but a weight on our conscience and distraction in our hearts? Often a carefree journey brings a sorrowful return, and a fun evening makes a sad morning. All earthly joy begins pleasantly, but in the end it steals and destroys. What can we see in the world that we cannot see at home? Look at the heavens, the earth, and the elements, for all of these things are material and temporary.

What can we see anywhere that will last long under the sun? We may believe things of earth will satisfy, but we will never attain fulfillment in them. If we could see the whole world at once, what would we have but a futile vision? Let us lift up our eyes to God on high and pray that our sins of action and inaction may be forgiven. We must leave worthless things to vain people and keep our minds on the things that God has commanded us. Let us shut the door behind us and call upon Jesus, our beloved. Remain with him in our room, for we will not find peace anywhere else. By not going out and listening to vain talk, we will keep ourselves in peace. But if we delight in hearing the latest news and gossip, we will not find peace for our hearts.

Book 1 Chapter 20

61

ON THE PEACE OF CHRIST

*Then you will experience God's peace, which exceeds
anything we can understand. His peace will
guard your hearts and minds as you live in Christ Jesus.*

Philippians 4:7

The Christ

My friend, I have said, "I am leaving you with a gift—peace
of mind and heart. And the peace I give is a gift the world
cannot give. So don't be troubled or afraid" (John 14:27).
Everyone wants peace, but not everyone cares for the things
which bring true peace. My peace comes to the humble
and lowly in heart. Your peace will be found in patience.
If you will hear me and follow my voice, you will enjoy
much peace.

The Disciple

What should I do then, Lord?

The Christ

In everything, concentrate on what you do and say. Then direct your purpose to this: do what pleases me alone. Do not desire or seek anything apart from me. And further more, don't judge others' words or deeds harshly. Don't meddle in matters that don't concern you, then you will be rarely disturbed. Don't dwell on things that upset you and cause you to suffer physically or emotionally, but keep an eternal perspective. My peace doesn't depend on feeling no anxiety, things going well, having no adversity, or things working out according to your wishes. And don't think you are anything great or think that you are especially loved if you are in a joyful and delightful mood. It is not by these things that your true love for righteousness is known, nor do these things benefit or perfect you.

The Disciple

In what then, Lord?

The Christ

In offering yourself with all your heart to my divine will. In not seeking things which aren't your own: whether great or small, temporal or eternal. You can maintain a steady state in giving thanks in both adversity and prosperity. Consider them the same in my care. You will walk in truth and the way of peace if you are so brave and patient in hope that when inward comfort is taken from you, you prepare your heart for more endurance; if you don't justify yourself as if you shouldn't have to suffer heavy burdens; and if you don't judge me for the things I appoint for you; and if you bless my holy name. Then you will have a sure hope that you again will see my face filled with joy for you. Then you will enjoy an abundance of peace, as much as possible among fallen people.

Book 3 Chapter 25

62

ON PEACE TO BE SOUGHT
IN GOD ALONE

*Now may the God of peace make you holy in every way,
and may your whole spirit and soul and body
be kept blameless until our Lord Jesus Christ comes again.*

1 Thessalonians 5:23

The Disciple

Whatever we desire or imagine for our comfort, we will
not find here, but only in the hereafter. If we had all the
comforts of this world and were able to enjoy all its pleasure, it is certain it would not last long. Here, our souls
cannot be fully comforted and perfectly refreshed except
in God. He is the comforter of the poor and the exalter
of the humble. If we wait for the divine promise, in just a
little while, we will have an abundance of all good things in
heaven. If we long too much for the things that are temporal, we will lose those things which are eternal. Use earthly
things, but desire eternal things. We cannot be satisfied

with any temporary good because we were not created to enjoy them.

Even if we had all good things which were ever created, we could not be happy and blessed. All our happiness and blessedness comes only from God who created all things. Happiness with things seems good to the foolish lover of the world. But, as Christ's good and faithful servants, "we are citizens of heaven, where the Lord Jesus Christ lives. And we are eagerly waiting for him to return as our Savior" (Philippians 3:20). All human comfort is empty and short-lived. Blessed and true is the comfort which resides inwardly and springs from the truth. Godly people every-where have within themselves the Comforter, Jesus, and say to him, "Be with me Lord Jesus, always and everywhere. Let my comfort come from giving up human comfort. And if I don't feel your comfort, let your will and righteous approval be my highest comfort. You are compassionate and merciful, slow to get angry and filled with unfailing love." The psalmist promises, God "will not constantly accuse us, nor remain angry forever'" (Psalm 103:9).

Book 3 Chapter 16

63

ON SEEKING PEACE OF MIND

"I am leaving you with a gift—peace of mind and heart.
And the peace I give is a gift the world cannot give.
So don't be troubled or afraid."

John 14:27

The Disciple

We may enjoy abundant peace if we will quit anxiously listening to who said what, who did what, and other things that don't concern us. How can we live in peace if we are occupying ourselves with other people's affairs and, meanwhile, paying little or no attention to our inner lives? Blessed are those whose hearts have a single focus on Christ, for they will have an abundance of peace.

How did saints become so perfect and contemplative of divine things? Because they earnestly sought to crucify themselves to all worldly desires. They were able to cling with their whole heart to God and so were free to have time to meditate on him. We are much too occupied with our own love and concern for temporary things. Also, we seldom overcome even a single sin and are not eager to grow in grace. And so we remain half-hearted and unspiritual.

If we would be watchful of ourselves, and if our spirit were not bound to outward things, then we might be wise about salvation and make progress in understanding divine truth. Our great and terrible failure is that we are not free from our earthly loves and desires. We do not strive for holy perfection. So, when even a little trouble comes our way, we are too easily discouraged and rush to the world for comfort.

If we would reject our own desires and stand firm in battle, then we would see the Lord helping us from heaven. For he himself is always ready to help those strive to be like him and trust in him. He even provides opportunities to struggle, so in the end we may win the victory. If we judge our spiritual progress by only outward observances and rituals, our devotion will soon come to an end.

But we must take an ax to the very roots of our life and chop out all earthly entanglements so we may possess peace in our souls.

If each year, we could take the ax to a fault, we would quickly grow into spiritual perfection. But to the contrary, we often feel that we were better and holier in our lifestyle years earlier in our Christian life. Enthusiasm and progress in our spiritual journey must increase day after day. Yet, now it seems a great thing if we can retain some portion of our first love (Revelation 2:4). If we put in a slight effort in the beginning, then as we grow we should be able to do all things with ease and joy.

It is a hard thing to break through a habit, and harder yet to overcome our own desires. But if you can't overcome slight and easy obstacles, how will you overcome greater ones? Let us resist our human will and unlearn evil habits at the beginning of our spiritual journey, so that it doesn't lead us into worse difficulties. Oh, if we knew what peace a holy life would bring to us and what joy it would bring to others, we would be more eager for spiritual progress.

Book 1 Chapter 11

64

ON FOUR THINGS WHICH
BRING GREAT PEACE

"I have told you all this so that you may have peace in me.
Here on earth you will have many trials and sorrows.
But take heart, because I have overcome the world."

John 16:33

The Christ

My friend, now I will teach you the way of peace and true
freedom.

The Disciple

My Lord, do as you say, because I am eager to hear.

The Christ

Strive, my friend, to do another's will rather than your own.
Always choose to have less than more. Always seek after
the least honorable place and be under all authority. Always
wish and pray that you will fulfill God's will for you. If

you do this, you will receive an inheritance of peace and tranquility.

The Disciple

O my Lord, your short lesson is perfect. It is short in words, but long in meaning and abundant in application. If it were possible for me to fully live it out, I would not be so easily disturbed with evil thoughts and desires. When I find myself anxious and depressed, I find that I've gone against this teaching. But you, who are the Almighty and love to see me make progress in my soul, grant more grace that I may be able to fulfill your command and work out my salvation.

"O God, don't stay away. My God, please hurry to help me" (Psalm 71:12).

You have said, "I will go before you . . . and level the mountains" (Isaiah 45:2). You will open the heavenly doors of knowledge and reveal your secrets.

Lord, do as you say, and let all evil thoughts fly away in your presence. This is my hope and my only comfort: to fly away to you during troubled times, to hope in you, to call upon you from my heart, and patiently wait for your loving kindness.

Enlighten me, Blessed Jesus, with the brightness of your inner light, and eliminate all darkness from every corner of my heart. Restrain my many wandering thoughts and overcome the temptations that intend to harm me. You fight fiercely for me and drive away the evil beasts of lust. "May there be peace within your walls and prosperity in your palaces" (Psalm 122:7). May my conscience be pure. You command the winds and the storms and say to the sea, "Be still." You tell the stormy wind, "Hold your peace," and there is great calm.

"Send out your light and your truth" (Psalm 43:3). May they shine upon the earth. I am only earth without form and void until you give me light. Pour out your grace from above. Baptize my heart with the water of grace. Give your waters of devotion to refresh the face of the earth and cause it to bring forth good and perfect fruit. Buoy up my mind which is weighed down with heavy sins. Lift my thoughts and desires to heavenly things. I have tasted the sweet happiness which comes from above, so may I not take any pleasure in thinking about things of the earth.

Draw me to yourself and deliver me from unstable creature comforts, for no created thing is able to satisfy my desires and give me comfort. May I be one with you in an inseparable bond of love. You alone are sufficient to those who love you. Without you, all things are unfulfilling toys.

Book 3 Chapter 23

65

ON WHAT MAKES
A PEACEABLE PERSON

*The Holy Spirit produces this kind of fruit in
our lives: love, joy, peace, patience, kindness, goodness,
faithfulness, gentleness, and self-control.*

Galatians 5:22-23

The Disciple

If we are at peace with ourselves, then we will be able to
be peacemakers with others. A peaceable person does
more good than a well-educated person. People ruled by
their emotions turn even good into evil and easily believe
the worst. Good, peaceable people turn all things into
good. They are not suspicious of anyone, but people who
are discontented and restless are tossed about with much
paranoia. They are neither quiet, nor do they tolerate others
who are quiet. They often say things they shouldn't say and
don't know the right things. They are quick to point out
rules that should be followed, but they themselves neglect

those rules. So, we must first work eagerly on our own spiritual lives. Only then can we help our neighbors in their spiritual lives.

We know well how to excuse and justify our own actions, but we won't accept the excuses of others. It would be better to accuse ourselves and excuse others. If we want others to be patient with us, then we must be patient with others. Let us be aware just how far we are from true love and humility, which doesn't become angry or indignant against anyone but itself. It's no great thing to associate with the good and kind, since that is naturally pleasing to all. Everyone of us enjoys peace with people who think well of us. But to be able to live peaceably with difficult, stubborn, and disorderly people or those who oppose us requires great grace. To do this is most worthy and commendable.

Some people keep peace with themselves, and so keep themselves in peace. Other people don't have peace nor allow others to have peace. They are troublesome to others, but are actually more trouble to themselves. Others control themselves in peace and work to bring others peace. Nevertheless, all our peace in this sad life lies in humble suffering rather than not feeling adversity. People who know best how to suffer will possess the most peace. Those people are conquerors of themselves and lords of their world, the friends of Christ, and the inheritors of heaven.

Book 2 Chapter 3

66

ON PEACE THAT DOESN'T DEPEND ON PEOPLE

*You adulterers! Don't you realize that friendship
with the world makes you an enemy of God?
I say it again: If you want to be a friend of the world,
you make yourself an enemy of God.*

James 4:4

The Christ

If you depend on friends of whom you have a high opinion to give you peace, you will be disappointed with a disturbed spirit. But if you depend on me, the ever-living and indwelling Truth, the desertion or death of a friend will not cause you to lose your peace. The love of your friend should come from me. For my sake, everyone is to be loved even if they don't seem dear or advantageous to you. Without me, friendships have no strength or endurance. If I am not in it, love is never true or pure. You ought to be so dead to the human affections of beloved friends that you could live without their companionship. The closer you come to me, the farther you distance yourself from all earthly support. And the deeper you look into yourself, the more wretched you appear in your own eyes and the higher you ascend toward God.

But people who attribute good to themselves, hinder the grace of God from coming to them, because the Holy Spirit is seeking to dwell in a humble heart. If you could consider yourself utterly nothing and empty yourself of the love of every created thing or person, then I would flow into you with great grace. When you set your eyes on created things, the face of the Creator turns from you. In all things, learn to conquer your earthly desires for your Creator's sake. Then you will be able to attain divine knowledge. No matter how small something may be, if you love it more than me, it will corrupt you and hold you back from receiving the highest good.

Book 3 Chapter 42

67

ON A PURE MIND AND SIMPLE INTENTIONS

*Fix your thoughts on what is true, and honorable,
and right, and pure, and lovely, and admirable.
Think about things that are excellent and worthy of praise.*

Philippians 4:8

The Disciple

Two wings lift people above earthly things: simplicity and purity. Simplicity should be our motivation; purity our goal. Simplicity reaches toward God; purity brings us into relationship. No good action will be distasteful to you if you are free from wrong desires. You will find inward freedom if you seek and reach after nothing but the will of God and the good of your neighbor. If your heart is right, then every creature is a mirror of life and a book of holy doctrine. There is no creature too small or evil that it doesn't reveal to us the goodness of God.

If you are good and pure within, then you can look upon all things without sorrow or misunderstanding. A pure heart sees the very depths of heaven and hell. As you are inwardly, so you judge outwardly. If there is any joy in the world, surely those with a pure heart possess it. And if there is trouble and anguish, the one with an evil conscience knows it best. As iron cast into the fire loses its rust and is refined, so the people who turn themselves completely to God are freed of laziness and changed into new people.

When people become half-hearted spiritually, they fear even the smallest labor and willingly accept outward comfort. But when people begin to conquer themselves and to walk bravely in the way of God, then they count those things as nothing which in the past were so troubling to them.

Book 2 Chapter 4

68

ON THE INSTABILITY
OF OUR HEARTS

"The human heart is the most deceitful of all things,
and desperately wicked. Who really knows how bad it is?
But I, the LORD, search all hearts and
examine secret motives."

Jeremiah 17:9-10

The Christ

My friend, do not trust feelings, since what you are feeling now will quickly change into something opposite. As long as you live, you are unwillingly subject to change. Now you are joyful, now sad; now at peace, now anxious; now devoted, now fickle; now disciplined, now careless. But wise people—those who are truly acquainted with the Spirit—stand above changeable things. They don't concentrate on what they may be feeling or from which direction the wind may be blowing. Their minds are intently focused on those things that will carry them to their desired end. So, they are able to remain one and same, unshaken, with their eyes firmly fixed on me despite the many changes in the world.

If you are intent and pure in your focus, you will travel safely through many storms. But if your focus becomes dim and impure, it will quickly find rest on anything that seems pleasant, for it is self-seeking. "When all the people heard of [my] arrival, they flocked to see . . . Lazarus, the man [I] had raised from the dead" (John 12:9). Focus your eyes on *me* rather than whatever comes your way.

Book 3 Chapter 33

69

ON THE JOY OF
A GOOD CONSCIENCE

Keep your conscience clear. Then if people speak against you,
they will be ashamed when they see what
a good life you live because you belong to Christ.

1 Peter 3:16

The Disciple

The glory of a good person is the testimony of a good conscience. If you have a good conscience, you will have joy forever. A good conscience can bear much trouble and is extremely joyful in the midst of adversities. But an evil conscience is always fearful and anxious. You will rest soundly if your heart doesn't condemn you. Don't rejoice, unless you have done good. God has said, "But those who still reject me are like the restless sea, which is never still but continually churns up mud and dirt. There is no peace for the wicked" (Isaiah 57:20-21). And if they say, "We are in peace and no harm will happen to us. Who would dare to hurt us?" don't believe them. For suddenly all the wrath of God will rise against them, and their deeds will be brought to nothing. Even their thoughts will disappear.

Loving people don't grieve in trouble but glory in it, for such rejoicing comes from finding glory in the cross of Christ. Glory that comes from the world lasts only briefly. Sadness always goes hand in hand with the glory of the world. The glory in good people comes from a clear conscience and not in the opinions of others. The joy of the upright is from God and *in* God; their joy is in the truth.

People who desire true and eternal glory don't care about temporary things. People who seek temporary glory despise eternal glory and reveal in their hearts little love for heavenly things. People who don't care about human praise or criticism have great peace in their hearts.

Those people with a pure conscience will be easily contented and filled with peace. They feel no more holy when they are praised or more sinful when they are criticized. We are what we are, and we can be no better than what God judges us to be. If we consider well what we are inwardly, we will not care what people say about us outwardly. "The LORD doesn't see things the way you see them. People judge by outward appearance, but the LORD looks at the heart" (1 Samuel 16:7). A humble spirit's character is to always do right and give little thought to itself. A sign of great purity and inward faithfulness is not looking for comfort from any created thing.

People looking for outward signs to judge their lives, show plainly that they are not wholly committed to God. People who commend themselves are not approved by God. St. Paul writes, "When people commend themselves, it doesn't count for much. The important thing is for the Lord to commend them" (2 Corinthians 10:18). To walk inwardly with God—and not be held by outward loves—is the state of a spiritual person.

Book 2 Chapter 6

70

ON PREPARING OUR HEARTS
FOR THE LORD'S SUPPER

*For if you eat the bread or drink the cup without honoring
the body of Christ, you are eating and drinking
God's judgment upon yourself.*

1 Corinthians 11:29

The Christ

Diligently examine your conscience with all your might.
Cleanse and purify it with true repentance and humble confession. Then you will feel no burden or remorse
that will hinder your free approach to God. Be especially
sorrowful and mournful for your daily shortcomings.
Confess to God the secrets of your heart and all the shortcomings in your love for me.

Deeply grieve and be sorry because you are still driven
by desires that are sinful and worldly. Your desires and
drives are not dead, so you are often entangled in fruitless
fantasies; influenced by outward things, but so neglectful

of internal things; so ready to laugh and take life lightly, but not ready for weeping and repentance; so prone to be lazy and prone to earthly desires, but so dull to zeal and enthusiasm; so curious to hear novel ideas and eager to seek earthly beauty, but so unwilling to be humble and despised; so greedy for material things, so grudging toward giving, so materialistic; so inconsiderate in speaking, so reluctant to keep silence; so disorderly in manners, so inconsiderate in action; so desirous for food, but having no appetite for the Word of God; so eager to rest, but so slow to labor; so eager to hear gossip, but so lazy toward holy disciplines and so eager for the end of them, so distracted, so negligent in observing the hours of prayer; so half-hearted in praising God, but so quick to become angry; so displeased at others, so prone to judging, so severe in correction; so joyful in prosperity, so weak in adversity; being good at resolutions, but so bad in keeping them.

When you have confessed and wept over these and other shortcomings, and when you have been grieved and displeased at your sin, then determine to continually change your actions and attitudes while making progress in living a good life. Then, with full submission and your entire will, honor my name on the altar of your heart as a perpetual burnt offering. As you faithfully present your body and soul to me, may you be considered worthy to draw near to me and offer this sacrifice of praise and thanksgiving. Receive the sacrament of my body and blood to your soul's health. For their is no ritual worthier, no greater satisfaction than the destroying of sin in the act of Holy Communion. If people will do what they can and truly repent, then they will draw close to me for pardon and grace. As I live, I say, "Do you think that I like to see wicked people die? . . . Of course not! I want them to turn from their wicked ways and live" (Ezekiel 18:22-23).

Book 4 Chapter 7

71

ON THE EXERCISES OF
A RIGHTEOUS PERSON

Supplement your faith with a generous provision of
moral excellence, and moral excellence with knowledge,
and knowledge with self-control, and self-control with
patient endurance, and patient endurance with godliness,
and godliness with brotherly affection, and brotherly affection
with love for everyone. The more you grow like this,
the more productive and useful you will be in
your knowledge of our Lord Jesus Christ.

2 Peter 1:5-8

The Disciple

Our Christian life should be demonstrated with all virtues,
so that our inward and outward behavior should be the
same. Our inner attitudes should be even better than our
outward actions, because God looks at our hearts. We must
reverence him with all our hearts wherever we are and walk
purely in his presence as do the angels. We should daily

renew our commitment to God and rekindle the zeal of our hearts as if each day were the first day of our conversion. Pray, "Help me, O God, in my good resolutions and in your holy service. Grant today I make a good beginning, for up to this point, I have done nothing!"

Our rate of spiritual progress depends on our commitment. Much diligence is needed to make good progress. If we resolve bravely and then fall short, how will it be with those who never resolve or do so feebly? But many things cause us to abandon our commitment, yet just a trivial lack of holy disciplines can cause us to lose our resolve. Our commitment depends more on the grace of God than upon our own wisdom. We must trust him with everything we have. "I know, LORD, that our lives are not our own. We are not able to plan our own course" (Jeremiah 10:23).

If a holy habit is sometimes not done for the sake of a greater good or human kindness, we can easily resume it afterward. But if we neglect spiritual exercises through dislike or laziness, then it is sinful and will lead to trouble. Let us strive as earnestly as we can, so we will not sin. We should always resolve to live righteous lives, but most of all strive to overcome sins that so easily trip us up. Both our outer and inner lives must be strictly examined and disciplined, because both are necessary to our progress.

If we can't be constantly examining ourselves, we *can* at

certain times such as morning and evening. In the morning, we can make our resolution to imitate Christ and at evening examine how we have done in word, deed, and thought. Have we offended God or our neighbor in any of these areas? We must prepare our minds and bodies to repel the assaults of the devil. Let us control our appetites, and we will soon be able to control every human desire. Always have something good to do: read, write, pray, meditate, or do something helpful for the community. Be careful about bodily exercise, for not every workout is right for everyone.

Spiritual exercises should not be done publicly, but are best to be done in private. But we must not neglect our public duties any more than our secret responsibilities. Let us be faithful and trustworthy to complete our duties and the requirements assigned to us. Then, once they are completed, and we still have time, do whatever God seems to direct us to do. Everyone cannot have the same spiritual exercises, but some disciplines are helpful to this person and another to that person. For different seasons in life different disciplines are appropriate, such as feasting and fasting. Sometimes we grow more through temptations and other times through peace and quietness. Some spiritual exercises are suitable for times of sadness, while others are best when we are joyful in the Lord.

Book 1 Chapter 19

72

ON THE READING OF
THE HOLY SCRIPTURES

*All Scripture is inspired by God and is useful to teach us
what is true and to make us realize what is
wrong in our lives. It corrects us when we are
wrong and teaches us to do what is right.*

2 Timothy 3:16

The Disciple

We must look for truth in the Holy Bible, not curious concepts. All Scripture should be read in the spirit in which it was written. We must first search for what is profitable for our own spiritual lives rather than mining Scripture for a sermon, talk, or Bible study. We ought to read simple devotional books as well as those that are deep and difficult.

Do not let the writer's authority or learning—be it little or great—influence you, but let the love of pure truth attract you to read. Do not ask, "Who said this?" but pay attention to what is said.

People pass away, but the truth of the Lord endures forever. God speaks in many ways to everyone without respect of persons. Our own curiosity often hinders us in the reading of holy writings when we simply want to discuss and debate issues. Avoid these discussions. If you want to read for your spiritual profit, read humbly, simply, honestly, and not to impress people with your knowledge. Don't be afraid to ask questions and listen in silence to the words of godly people. Don't be displeased at criticism from people who have been Christians longer than you, for there is a reason for their advice.

Book 1 Chapter 5

73

ON THE DISCIPLINE OF
RELIGIOUS LIFE

All athletes are disciplined in their training.
They do it to win a prize that will fade away,
but we do it for an eternal prize. So I run with
purpose in every step. I am not just shadowboxing.
I discipline my body like an athlete,
training it to do what it should.

1 Corinthians 9:25-27

The Disciple

It is beneficial to us to die to many personal desires if we want to live in love and harmony with other people. It is no small thing to live in a religious community or church without complaining and to remain faithful to the group until death. Blessed are the ones who have lived a good life in such a group and remained faithful even until death. If we want to stand firm and grow in our faith, we must consider ourselves as an exile and pilgrim upon the earth. If we lead a holy life, we will be considered as a fool for Christ (1 Corinthians 4:10).

Our clothing and outward appearance are not very important, but our change in character and complete death to earthly desires is what make us holy people. If we seek only to serve God for the health of our soul, we will find only troubles, trials, and sorrow. People who live long in peace strive to be the least of all and servant to all.

We are called to endure and to work hard, not to live a life of ease and careless talk. Here on earth, we are refined as gold in the furnace. We cannot endure, unless with all our hearts we humble ourselves for God's sake.

Book 1 Chapter 17

74

ON THE INEVITABILITY
OF TEMPTATION

*[Jesus] understands our weaknesses, for he faced
all of the same testings we do, yet he did not sin.
So let us come boldly to the throne of our gracious God.
There we will receive his mercy, and
we will find grace to help us when we need it most.*

Hebrews 4:15-16

The Disciple

Blessed be your name forever, O Lord, who has allowed this
temptation and trouble. We cannot escape it, but we need
to flee to you that you may encourage us and turn it for our
good (Romans 8:28). Lord, I am in serious trouble, things
are not well in my heart, and I am very troubled by the
suffering that weighs upon me. And now, O dear Father,
I say with your Son, "Now my soul is deeply troubled.
Should I pray, 'Father, save me from this hour'"? (John
12:27). May we be glorified when we are terribly humbled

and be delivered through your power. "Please, LORD, rescue me! Come quickly, LORD, and help me" (Psalm 40:13). What can we poor people do, and where can we go? Give us also patience. Help us, O Lord my God, and we will not fear no matter how we are weighed down.

So, during this time of temptation, what will we say? Lord, your will be done. We truly deserve to be troubled and weighed down. So, we should bear this with patience until the storm is past and comfort returns. Your power is able to take this temptation away from us and to lessen its power, so we are not crushed under it even as you have rescued us many times in the past. O God, merciful God, my merciful God, as difficult as being delivered from the temptation is, it is easy for your mighty hand.

Book 3 Chapter 29

75

ON NO SECURITY
IN THIS LIFE

The LORD says, "I will rescue those who love me.
I will protect those who trust in my name.
When they call on me, I will answer;
I will be with them in trouble."

Psalm 91:14

The Christ

My friend, you are never secure in this life, so you will need
your spiritual armor for as long as you live. You live among
the enemy and are attacked on the right and left. Use your
shield of faith on all sides, and you will remain unharmed.
Beware, if you don't keep your heart focused on me with
steadfast purpose, you will not survive the fierceness of the
attack nor attain the victory of the blessed. So, struggle
bravely all through your life and strike with a strong hand
those that oppose you. "To everyone who is victorious I

will give some of the manna that has been hidden away in heaven" (Revelation 2:17). But great misery is reserved for the lazy.

If you seek rest in this life, how will you attain eternal rest? Don't strive for more rest, but more patience. Seek the true peace which is found only in God in heaven— not on earth or in created things. For the love of God, you must willingly bear all things: labors or sorrows, temptations, frustrations, anxieties, necessities, illnesses, injuries, conflicts, rebukes, humiliation, confusion, corrections, and disrespect. These things build righteous character, prove you are my disciple, and fashion your heavenly crown. I will give you an everlasting reward for temporary labor, infinite glory for short-lived shame.

Don't think you will always have spiritual comforts whenever you wish. My saints never sought comfort, but instead bore much grief, many temptations, and heavy despair. But they bore all these things and trusted in God more than in themselves. They knew that the suffering of this present time is nothing compared to our future glory. "In fact, together with [me, you] are heirs of God's glory. But if [you] are to share [my] glory, [you] must also share [my] suffering" (Romans 8:17). This glory is not attained immediately, but only after many tears and hard labor. Wait for my reward and be strong. Do not be faint of heart nor stray from my path. Constantly glorify me with your body and soul. I will richly reward you as we together go through your troubles. You are my child and my heir.

Book 3 Chapter 35

76

ON RESISTING TEMPTATION

*The temptations in your life are no different from
what others experience. And God is faithful.
He will not allow the temptation to be
more than you can stand.
When you are tempted, he will show you
a way out so that you can endure.*

1 Corinthians 10:13

The Disciple

As long as we live in the world we will always face troubles
and trials. So, it is written, "Is not all human life a struggle?"
(Job 7:1). We must be aware of these trials and troubles—
and pray. The devil is always looking for an opportunity to
deceive. He never sleeps and goes about seeking for someone he can devour (1 Peter 5:8). People are never so perfect
in holiness that they never have temptation, nor can they be
completely free from them.

However, temptations can turn into great benefits. Through them we are humbled, purified, and instructed. All saints have endured many troubles and trials and temptation, yet have grown through them. Those who have not endured temptation become good for nothing and fall away. There is no state so sacred, no place so secure that it is without temptations and troubles.

We are never completely free from temptations for as long as we live, we have the root of temptation within us since we were born in sin. One temptation or sorrow passes away and another takes its place. We all have to suffer because we haven fallen from perfect happiness. Many people who try to flee from temptations fall more deeply into them. We cannot overcome simply by fleeing, but by endurance and true humility we are made stronger than all our enemies.

To only resist temptation outwardly and not pull it up by the root, doesn't benefit much, but temptations will return quickly and will become worse. With the help of God himself—not our own strength and strain—little by little, through patience and determination, we will conquer all. In the midst of temptation, regularly seek godly advice. Don't deal severely with those who are tempted, but comfort and strengthen them as you would like to be treated.

The root of all temptation springs from an unstable

spirit and a lack of trust in God. For just as ships without helms are tossed about by the waves, so are people who are careless and lacking purpose: now on this side, now on that side. As fire tests iron, so does temptation refine the upright person. We rarely know how strong we are until temptation reveals our strength. So, we must fight, especially at the beginning of temptation, when the foe is more easily defeated. Don't allow the enemy to enter your mind, but meet him outside the door as soon as he knocks. Someone has warned:

> You failed at the start, when it could have been cured,
> It's now past your skill, too long it's endured.

Temptation first comes to our minds with a simple suggestion, then strong imagination. This is followed by pleasure, evil desires, and then consent. So, little by little, the enemy enters in because he was not resisted at the beginning. The longer we delay our resistance, the weaker we grow, and the stronger the enemy's power against us becomes.

Many people suffer their most intense temptation soon after coming to Christ, while others face it at the end of life. Some are severely tested their entire life. Some people are tempted lightly according to the wisdom and justice of God, who knows the character and circumstances of each person and works all for the good of his children (Romans 8:28).

So, we shouldn't despair when we are tempted, but we should more fervently cry out to Christ. He will help us in all our troubles and trials. As St. Paul wrote, "The temptations in your life are no different from what others experience. And God is faithful. He will not allow the temptation to be more than you can stand. When you are tempted, he will show you a way out so that you can endure" (1 Corinthians 10:13). Humble yourself under the mighty hand of God in all temptation and trouble, for he will save and lift you up if you are a humble person.

People are proven in temptations and troubles by the progress they make. Those who overcome become more righteous and their reward is great. It's no great thing if we are devout and zealous in our faith—as long as we suffer no troubles. But if we act patiently in times of great adversity, then there is hope for great progress. Some people are kept safe in great temptation, but are defeated in small and common temptations. But this will teach them not to trust to themselves in great things, because they are weak in small things.

Book 1 Chapter 13

77

ON HAVING
A SENSITIVE HEART

*Guard your heart above all else,
for it determines the course of your life.*

Proverbs 4:23

The Disciple

If you want to make spiritual progress, always respect God with holy reverence. And don't desire to be free, but restrain all your senses with discipline. Do not spend your time in senseless humor. If our hearts are sensitive to the Spirit, we will live a life devoted to God. This sensitivity opens the door to many good things, but a calloused heart will lead to great loss. It is wonderful that we can rejoice heartily in this life considering that we are pilgrims facing many dangers to our souls.

Through the lightness of our hearts and the denial of our shortcomings, without feeling sorrow in our souls, we vainly laugh when we have good reason to weep. There is no true liberty and real joy unless we reverence God with a good conscience. We are happy when we can cast away every source of distraction and serve the one purpose of holy sorrow over sin. We are happy when we remove anything that may strain or burden our conscience. Strive bravely. Bad habits are overcome with good habits. If we don't judge our work by other people's opinions, we are free to do our best work.

Let us not busy ourselves with the affairs of others, nor entangle ourselves with the affairs of famous people. We must always keep our eyes on ourselves first and give ourselves advice before giving it to our dearest friends. If we don't have favor with people, don't be discouraged. Instead, let us be concerned about wisely conducting ourselves as faithful servants of Christ. It's often better and safer for us not to have many comforts in this life, especially physical comforts. To our own blame, we don't seek divine comforts, because we don't seek repentance of heart. Instead, we cling to comforts that are fruitless and worldly.

We are all unworthy of divine comforts, but instead worthy of much trouble. When we are aligned with Christ, then all the world is burdensome and bitter to us. Good people will find sufficient cause for mourning and weeping. No one—neither ourselves nor our neighbors—live on this earth without trials and troubles. And the more we consider this, the more we grieve. Our sins and vices are grounds for deserved grief and inner sorrow. When we become so entangled with earthly things, we are seldom able to think on heavenly things.

If we would think about our own mortality and death more often, we would no doubt work harder to improve. And if we would seriously consider the torment of hell, I believe we would willingly endure toil, pain, and fear here on earth. But because these realities don't reach our hearts and minds, we continue to love pleasurable things and we remain spiritually cold and miserably indifferent.

Often, it is out of a poverty of the spirit, that our earthly bodies so easily complain. So, humbly pray to the Lord that he will give you the spirit of repentance, and say with the psalmist, "Don't raise your fists in defiance at the heavens or speak with such arrogance" (Psalm 75:5).

Book 1 Chapter 21

78

ON RESTRAINT OF OUR WORDS

People can tame all kinds of animals, birds, reptiles,
and fish, but no one can tame the tongue.
It is restless and evil, full of deadly poison.
Sometimes it praises our Lord and Father, and sometimes
it curses those who have been made in the image of God.

James 3:7-9

The Disciple

Avoid, as much as you can, people's drama. Talk of worldly
things, though innocent enough, is a hindrance as it quickly
becomes a habit and leads to meaningless chatter. Many
times I wish I had held my peace and avoided going out
among people. Why do we continually talk and gossip, since
we seldom resume our silence without harm to our conscience? We like talking so much because we hope, by our
conversation, to gain some comfort or refresh our wearied
spirit with our words. We are very willing to talk and think
about things which we love and those things we hate.

But often our conversation is fruitless with no good purpose. The outward comfort on conversation is a huge hindrance to the inner comfort which comes only from God. So, we must watch and pray that we do not idle away our time. If it is right and desirable to speak, speak only things which build up yourself and others. Evil habits and ignoring what is of real value causes us not to watch our words. Nevertheless, holy conversation on spiritual things helps us in our spiritual progress. Those with kindred minds and spirits find their common ground in fellowship with God.

Book 1 Chapter 10

79

ON AVOIDING GOSSIP

*Avoid worthless, foolish talk that only leads
to more godless behavior.*

2 Timothy 2:16

The Christ

My friend, do not be curious about others or trouble
yourself with fruitless cares. "What is that to you?" (John
21:22). For what is it to you if people do this or that or say
thus and thus? You're not required to have an answer for
others, but you must give an answer for yourself. So why do
you entangle yourself with others' lives? I know all people
and observe all that they do under the sun. I know the condition of all people and know what they think, what they
desire, and how high or low their thoughts reach. All things,
then, are under my authority. So determine to live in godly
peace and allow disagreeable people to be as disagreeable
as they wish.

Do not seek after popular people. Do not try to be friends with many people. And do not be concerned about how much you are loved. These things breed distractions and great sorrows of your heart. If you will diligently look for my presence and open to me the gates of your heart, I will freely speak to you and reveal my secrets. "Be earnest and disciplined in your prayers" (1 Peter 4:7). Humble yourself in all things.

Book 3 Chapter 24

80

ON HUMAN NATURE AND GRACE

*Those who are dominated by the sinful nature think
about sinful things, but those who are controlled by the
Holy Spirit think about things that please the Spirit.
So letting your sinful nature control your mind leads
to death. But letting the Spirit control
your mind leads to life and peace.*

Romans 8:5-6

The Christ

My friend, pay strict attention to the workings of human
nature and grace. They subtly move in opposite directions
and are hard to distinguish unless you are spiritual and inwardly perceptive. All people try to look good and appear
to be good in all they say and do, but their "goodness" can
be deceiving.

Human nature is deceitful and distracts, it entraps
and deceives many people, and it always has selfish motives. But grace walks in simplicity and turns away from

every appearance of evil. It does not put on a false facade, but does everything entirely for the sake of God. Grace is submissive and bears its responsibilities willingly. Grace dies to selfish desires and resists sensuality. Grace-filled people seek to be disciplined, seek to be submissive, long to be under authority, and don't want to take advantage of their freedom. Grace loves to be held accountable and not to dominate anyone, but always to live under the authority of God, and—for the sake of God—submits to the human law.

Nature strives for its own advantage and looks at people, considering what it can gain from them. Grace considers not what is useful or convenient to itself, but what will benefit many people.

Nature eagerly accepts honor and reverence. Grace directs all honor and glory to God.

Nature fears shame and contempt. Grace rejoices in humiliation for the name of Jesus.

Nature loves leisure and bodily rest. Grace cannot be idle and gladly embraces hard work.

Nature desires to have what is new and attractive and hates those things that are not sophisticated and seemingly without value. Grace is delighted with simple and humble things, and doesn't despise common things. It doesn't refuse to wear old clothes.

Nature highly regards temporary things, rejoices in earthly riches, becomes sad with loss, and is upset by any hurtful word. Grace strives for things that are eternal and doesn't cling to temporary things. It is not upset by losses, nor embittered by hard words. Grace has placed its treasure and joy in heaven where it will never die.

Nature is greedy and more willing to receive than give. It loves things that are personal and private to itself. Grace, meanwhile, is kind and generous, avoids selfishness, is content with little, and believes it is more blessed to give than to receive.

Nature focuses on created things, its own body, selfish desires, and debauchery. Grace draws close to God and to righteousness. It avoids created things, flees the world, hates the desires of the body, avoids unstable things, and blushes to be in the public eye.

Nature is glad to receive delightful and sensuous creature comforts. Grace seeks to be comforted by God alone and to delight in good above all visible things.

Nature does everything for its own gain and profit, refuses to do anything freely as a favor, but is always hoping to find something good or better, seeks favor and praise for its good deeds, and longs to have its own deeds and gifts be highly praised. Grace seeks nothing temporary nor requires any reward apart from God alone. It doesn't seek earthly necessities, but only those things that lead to eternal life.

Nature rejoices in having many friends and family members. It boasts of noble birth and the exotic places it has been. It smiles at the powerful, flatters the rich, applauds people like itself. Grace loves even its enemies. It is not lifted by its many friends. It puts no value on where it was born or where it lives—unless there is more eternal goodness in it. Grace favors the poor more than the rich person, has more sympathy toward innocent people than the powerful. It rejoices with the truthful person, not the liar. Grace always encourages good people to seek after better spiritual gifts. It has become holy like the Son of God.

Nature is quick to complain of poverty and trouble. Grace constantly bears poverty.

Nature looks at all things from its own perspective, and strives and argues for itself. Grace credits God for all good things rather than arrogantly assigning any good to itself. It is not contentious nor argues its opinions are better than others. But in every sense and thought, grace submits itself to eternal wisdom and divine judgment.

Nature is eager to hear secrets and know the latest gossip. It loves to go abroad and experience many sensual pleasures. It seeks to be acknowledged and to do things which garner praise and admiration. Grace doesn't care that there is nothing new or lasting upon the earth. So it teaches others to restrain sensuality, to shun vain complacency and flamboyance, but to humbly hide those things that merit true praise and real admiration. With all knowledge it seeks useful fruit and the praise and honor of God. Grace doesn't seek to receive praise for its own self, but longs that God be blessed for his outpouring of pure, unadulterated love.

This grace is a supernatural life and a very special gift of God. It is the authentic mark of God's people and a promise of eternal salvation. It lifts up people from earthly things to the love of heavenly things. It makes a worldly person spiritual. So, as far as nature is completely pressed down and overcome, so much greater is grace which God pours out. Through grace, our inner beings are daily made into the image of God through fresh outpourings of the Spirit.

Book 3 Chapter 54

81

ON DESIRING ETERNAL LIFE

I'm torn between two desires: I long to go and
be with Christ, which would be far better for me.
But for your sakes, it is better that I continue to live.

Philippians 1:23-24

The Christ

My friends, fill your heart with my holy inspiration
that you may desire eternal happiness to be poured into
you from heaven above. May you long to depart from
this earthly body, that you may enjoy my presence without worldly shadows. Give me heart-felt thanks for my
supreme goodness and how I deal with you so graciously,
visit you so lovingly, inspire you so fervently, raise you up
so powerfully so you do not sink down to earthly things
under your own weight. It's not by your own meditating
and striving that you receive these gifts, but solely by the
gracious mercy of my supreme grace and divine care. Then

you will make progress in righteousness and humility as your prepare yourself for future conflicts. Cling to me with all the love in your heart and strive to serve me with an intense desire.

My friend, fire often burns with more smoke than flames. Likewise, the desires of some people burn toward heavenly things, yet they are not free from physical temptations. They are not on fire with pure and simple desire for God's glory when they pray. In the same way, sometimes you imagine you are praying earnestly and sincerely, but you are not pure or perfect, but praying out of your own selfish desires.

Don't seek things that are pleasant and advantageous to yourself, but only what is acceptable and honorable to me. For if you are to judge correctly, you must choose and follow after my plans rather than your own desire. I know your desires, and I have heard your pleas. You already long to enjoy the freedom of God's children. Already your eternal home delights you, and the heavenly country fills you with joy. But it is not time yet for you to go there. Stay here on earth for another season—even a season of warfare, labor, and testing. What you desire to be fulfilled with the greatest good cannot be attained immediately. I am that good right here. Wait for me until the kingdom of God will come.

You must still be tested with many trials here on earth. Heavenly comfort will be given to you from time to time, but abundant satisfaction will not be granted. So be strong and brave both in working with and overcoming your human nature. You must become a new person, being changed into another person. You must often do what your nature doesn't want to do and not do what your desires want to do. What pleases others will have good success; and what pleases you will have no success. What others say will be listened to; what you say will be paid no attention to. Others will ask and receive; you will ask and not obtain. Others will be great in the eyes of people; but about you, nothing will be spoken. To others this or that will be entrusted; you will be judged not trustworthy.

Because of this, you will sometimes be filled with sadness, but to bear these things silently is a great thing. In these and similar things, my faithful servants will be tested to see how far they will deny themselves and submit themselves to these slights. There is scarcely anything that is harder to deny and die to yourself than seeing others be elevated while you are commanded to do things which seem of little or no importance. And because you don't dare resist a higher power as yourself, it seems hard to chart your course according the desires of another and give up your own opinions.

But consider, my friend, the exceeding rewards for these brief earthly labors in my eternal kingdom. You will find no pain in bearing them, but rather the greatest satisfaction in patiently doing them. For in exchange for the trifling desires you have readily rejected, you will always have your will and desires in heaven. You will find there all you can desire and care for. There you will have all good things at your disposal with no fear of losing them. There you will be forever one with my will. You will desire no earthly or selfish things. No person will oppose you, no one will complain about you, no one will hinder you or stand in your path. There, all the things you desire will be present in one place and will refresh your whole being. You will be filled up to the brim. There, I will receive glory for the scorn I suffered on earth, I will provide a garment of praise for sorrow, and a throne in the kingdom from the lowest place. In heaven you will see the fruit of obedience, you will rejoice in your work of repentance, and your humble submission will be gloriously crowned.

But for now, humbly submit yourself to all people. Do not be troubled by who said this or who ordered that. But take special care that whenever your superior or equal or anyone requires something of you—or even shows a desire for something—do everything you can to fulfill their request. Let one person seek this, another seek that and be praised a million times. Rejoice in who you are in my own good pleasure and glory. Like St. Paul, say, "I trust that my life will bring honor to Christ, whether I live or die" (Philippians 1:20).

Book 3 Chapter 49

82

ON NOT TROUBLING OURSELVES WITH OUTWARD THINGS

Do not love this world nor the things it offers you,
for when you love the world, you do not have the love of
the Father in you. For the world offers only a craving for
physical pleasure, a craving for everything we see, and pride
in our achievements and possessions. These are not from
the Father, but are from this world. And this world is fading
away, along with everything that people crave. But anyone
who does what pleases God will live forever.

1 John 2:15-17

The Christ

My friend, it is beneficial to be ignorant and to consider yourself dead toward many things, as one crucified to the whole world. You must turn a deaf ear to many things. Instead, think on things that lead to peace. It is very profitable to turn away your eyes from things that are displeasing to me. Leave people to their own opinions, and avoid their arguments that lead to strife. If you are in a good relationship with God, and judge things by his mind, you will not be defeated.

The Disciple

O Lord, to what have we come? We mourn over temporal losses. We labor for trivial rewards. We hurry. We forget spiritual losses and rarely recover from these things. We seek after things that matter little, and we neglect those things that are absolutely essential. We will continue to slide down the slope toward material things until we come to our senses.

Book 3 Chapter 44

83

ON NOT LOVING THE WORLD

Jesus replied, "The Scriptures say, 'You must worship the LORD your God and serve only him.'"

Luke 4:8

The Disciple

Now I will speak again, O my Lord. I will not keep my peace. I will shout out to you, my God, my Lord, my King, who is exalted above all. "How great is the goodness you have stored up for those who fear you" (Psalm 31:19). What are you to those who love you? What are you to those who serve you with their whole hearts? It is unspeakably joyful to think about you and all that you pour out on those who love you. Most of all, you have shown me the depth of your love. You loved me before I was even born. You created me. And when I wandered far from you, you brought me back so I may serve you. You have commanded me to love you.

O fountain of perpetual love, what can I say about you? How can I not constantly think of you and how you lovingly remembered me—even when I ran away and nearly perished? You had mercy far beyond what your servant could have hoped for. You showed me your grace and friendship far beyond what I deserved. What can I possibly give in return for your grace? For you chose me to reject this world and its affairs, and take up a life of faith. It is such a great thing that I may serve you, whom every creature ought to serve. It is hard to comprehend such a great and wonderful thing that you have received one so poor and unworthy to be your servant and join with your other chosen servants.

Everything I have is yours, and with them I serve you. And yet, remarkably, you end up serving me instead! You have created heaven and earth to serve your people. Your creation obeys and daily performs whatever you command. You have even created the angels to serve your people. But above all these wonderful things, you have chosen to minister to your people and to give yourself to them.

What can I possibly give in return for your innumerable mercies? If I was only able to serve you every day of my life! Oh, if for only one day I could serve you in a worthy manner with honor and praise without end. Truly you are my God, and I am your poor servant who is bound to serve with all my strength. I wish I would never grow weary of praising you. This is my wish, my overwhelming desire. Please supply me with whatever is lacking to serve you.

It is a great honor and glory to serve you and to despise all earthly things for your sake. We, who submit ourselves to your most holy service, will have great grace. When we overcome every bodily delight we find the sweetest comfort of your Holy Spirit. When we enter the narrow way of life for your name's sake and put away earthly cares, we will attain great freedom in our spirits.

In our grateful and delightful service to you God, we are made truly free and holy! In your sacred religious service, we are made equal to the angels. We become well pleasing to you, acceptable to your faithful children, and terrifying to evil spirits. I delight in your service, which I desire and embrace. Your highest good is promised and joy will be forever more!

Book 3 Chapter 10

84

ON NOT RESTING ON
GOODS AND GIFTS

Send out your light and your truth; let them guide me.
Let them lead me to your holy mountain, to the place
where you live. There I will go to the altar of God,
to God—the source of all my joy. I will praise you
with my harp, O God, my God!

Psalm 43:3-4

The Disciple

Above all things and in all things, I always rest in you, O
Lord, for you are the eternal rest for your saints. Grant me,
most sweet and loving Jesus, to rest in you above every
person, above all health and beauty, above all glory and
honor, above all authority and dignity, above all knowledge
and skillfulness, above all riches and arts, above all joy and
exaltation, above all fame and praise, above all delights
and comfort, above all hope and promise, above all merit

and desire, above all gifts and rewards which you give and pour out, and above all joy and jubilation which my mind is able to receive and feel. You reign above angels and archangels, above the army of heaven, above all things visible and invisible, and above everything which you, O my God, are not.

For you, O Lord, my God, are the best above all things; you alone are the most high; you alone are the Almighty and all-comforting; you alone are completely lovely and loving; you alone are the most exalted and most glorious above all things, in whom all things are and were and forever will be, altogether and all-perfect. Everything you give me falls short and is insufficient without you. Whatever you reveal or promise me that is not revealed yet or fully possessed, is not sufficient. Truly my heart cannot fully rest and be content unless it rests in you. You satisfy beyond all gifts and anything people can offer.

O my most beloved Spouse, Jesus Christ, most holy lover of my soul, ruler of this whole creation, who but you can give me wings of true freedom that I may flee to you and find rest? When will I be given the openness to receive you fully, to see how sweet you are, O Lord my God? When can I bring my entire self to you, so that because of your love, I will not be aware of myself at all? May I wholly know you in ways that the world cannot. But now, I often groan and bear my sad condition with sorrow. Many evils confront me in this land of misery. They continually disturb me and fill me with sorrow. They hang like clouds that obscure the way and fill me with care. They seduce and entangle me, so I do not have free access to you. They keep me from enjoying sweet communion that is always available to your blessed disciples. Let my deep sighing come before you in my many troubles on earth.

O Jesus, Light of Eternal Glory, comfort my wandering soul. Before you, I am speechless, yet even my silence cries out to you. How long will you delay in making yourself known to me? Please come to me and make this poor, humble soul glad. Please put out your hand and deliver me from every trap. Please come, for without you there is no joyful day or hour. You are my joy, and without you my heart is empty. I am as miserable as a prisoner weighed down with shackles. Free me with the light of your presence, give me freedom, and reveal your loving character.

Let others seek pleasures instead of you, but for me nothing else pleases me except you. You are my God, my hope, and my eternal salvation. I will not hold my peace or cease to plead until I sense your grace return and you speak to my spirit.

The Christ
Look! Here I am. I have come to you because you called me. Your tears and longing of your soul, your humility and heart-felt sorrow have invited me and brought me to you.

The Disciple
And I replied, Lord, I have called to you and have longed to enjoy you. I was and am ready to reject everything for your sake. For you first called me to seek you. So, blessed be you, for you have brought this good work upon your servant according to your mercy. What then can your servant do in your presence except thoroughly humble himself to you by being always mindful of his wickedness and sinfulness? There is nothing to compare to you in all the wonders of heaven and earth. Your works are excellent, your judgments are true, and by your authority all things are governed. So, I give praise and glory to you, O Wisdom of the Father. Let my mouth, soul, and all created things praise and bless you together.

Book 3 Chapter 21

85

ON DELIGHT
ABOVE ALL THINGS

Taste and see that the LORD is good.
Oh, the joys of those who take refuge in him!

Psalm 34:8

The Disciple

Look! God is my all in all! What could I desire more? What additional happiness could I want? How delightful and satisfying you are, God. You warn, "Do not love this world nor the things it offers you, for when you love the world, you do not have the love of the Father in you" (1 John 2:15). God, you are my all! If we understand this, this is all we need to say. And to those who love it, it's pleasing to repeat it often. God, when you are present, everything is pleasant, but when you seem absent all things are exhausting. You give rest to our hearts as well as deep peace and festive joy. You make me consider all things correctly, and in everything I give you praise. Nothing can bring lasting pleasure without you. If anything is to be pleasant and satisfying, your grace must be there. Your wisdom fills every good thing.

If we taste your goodness, what can possibly be distasteful? To those who have not tasted your goodness, what can make them joyful? But those wise in the world's eyes and who enjoy physical pleasures do not have your true wisdom. Their "wisdom" will be found utterly futile, for to be human-minded is death. But those who follow after you—with contempt of earthly things and discipline of their bodies—will be found to be truly wise. They will be changed from futility to faithfulness, from earthly matters to the heavenly Spirit. They "taste and see that the LORD is good" (Psalm 34:8). Whatever good they find in other people, they give praise to the Creator. Unlike the created, the Creator enjoys eternity and light uncreated or reflected.

Lord of light everlasting, surpassing all created lights, beam down your rays from on high and enlighten the deepest parts of my heart. Give me purity, joy, clarity, and life to my spirit. May my spirit cling to you with joy that is greater than human understanding. When will that blessed and longed-for time come when you will satisfy with your presence and be everything I need? Until I sense your presence, my joy will not be complete. Still, unfortunately, my old human desires still live within me. They have not been fully crucified and are still very much alive. My desires still lust after my old nature and wage an inward war, keeping me from living in a peaceful kingdom.

But you, Jesus, who rules raging seas and stills the waves whenever they roar, rise up and help me. "Scatter the nations that delight in war" (Psalm 68:30). Destroy them by your power. Please show your might, and let your strong hand be glorified. I have no hope and refuge apart from you, my Lord and my God.

Book 3 Chapter 34

86

ON ENDURING TROUBLES FOR THE SAKE OF ETERNAL LIFE

In his kindness God called you to share in his eternal glory
by means of Christ Jesus. So after you have suffered
a little while, he will restore, support, and strengthen you,
and he will place you on a firm foundation.

1 Peter 5:10

The Christ

My friends, do not let the labors which you have undertaken for me break you down nor let trials and troubles cast you down in any way. I promise strength and comfort for you in every task. I am able to reward you above all measure and manner. You will not labor here long, and you will not always be weighed down with sorrows. Wait a little while, and you will see a quick end to evil. An hour is coming when all labor and conflict will cease. Time passes away very quickly.

Earnestly do your work and labor faithfully in my vineyard. I, myself, will be your reward. Write, read, sing, weep, be silent, pray, and bravely endure adversities. Eternal life is worth all these conflicts, yes, even greater. Peace will come at a day known only to the Lord. "There will be no normal day and night, for at evening time it will still be light" (Zechariah 14:7), but light eternal with infinite purity, steadfast peace, and undisturbed rest. You will not say then, "Who will free me from this life that is dominated by sin and death?" (Romans 7:24). You will not cry out, "Woe is me! My pilgrimage is prolonged." Death will be utterly destroyed. Salvation will never fail. There will be no anxiety, but only happy delight and a loving and noble society.

Oh, if you could see the saints crowned in eternal glory and hear the great praise they shout out. For they were treated contemptibly and unworthy of life. Then, truly you would immediately humble yourself to the earth and be willing to be subject to all those in authority over you. Nor would you long for pleasant days of this life, but would rejoice to be afflicted for God's sake. You would no longer seek to be esteemed by people.

Oh, if these things were desirable to you and moved you from the bottom of your heart, how could you ever complain again? Is not brief labor to be endured for the sake of eternal life? Losing or gaining the kingdom of God is no small thing. Lift up your face to heaven. Gaze on me and the saints with me, who in this world faced difficult conflict but now rejoice. They are now comforted, are now secure and at peace, and will remain with me forevermore in the kingdom of my father.

Book 3 Chapter 47

87

ON THE FREE SPIRIT

You will keep in perfect peace all who trust in you,
all whose thoughts are fixed on you!

Isaiah 26:3

The Disciple

Lord, the task of a perfect person is never to take their thoughts off heavenly things. Although they face many cares, they act as if they have no cares, not because they are indifferent, but because they are free from loving this world.

I plead with you, most merciful Lord God, to keep me from the cares of this life, so that I don't become too entangled in the necessities of my body and be taken captive by physical pleasure. Keep me from all things that prevent your Spirit from filling me, so that I won't be broken and discouraged with earthly cares. Not the cares that the world eagerly but vainly runs after, but the burden of simply being human that so often keep us from the freedom of the Spirit.

O my God, who gives me indescribable delight, turn to bitterness all the ways I seek satisfaction from bodily comfort and pleasure. These lure me away from the love of eternal things and wickedly draw me to some alluring delight. O my God, don't let flesh and blood have power over me. Do not let the world and its short-term glory deceive me. Don't let the enemy and his crafty lies deceive me. Give me courage to resist, patience to endure, and faithfulness to persevere. Grant, in place of all the creature comforts of this world, the sweet empowering of your Spirit, and in place of earthly affections, pour into me your eternal love.

Yes, food, drink, clothing, and other needs are necessary to this physical life, but they can be a distraction to living a spiritual life. Grant that I may use such things in moderation and that I will not be entangled with excessive love for them. We cannot live without our physical needs being met, but we must avoid unnecessary things which simply give delight or things that are forbidden by God's holy commandments. May we respect your Spirit with our physical bodies. Guide and teach me, O Lord, to avoid all excessive pleasures.

Book 3 Chapter 26

88

ON MEDITATING UPON DEATH

I press on to reach the end of the race and receive
the heavenly prize for which God,
through Christ Jesus, is calling us.

Philippians 3:14

The Disciple

Very quickly our life here will end. So, we must live very carefully knowing we will spend eternity in another world. People are here today and gone tomorrow. And, as quickly as they are out of sight, they are out of our minds. People's hearts can be so dull and hard, thinking only of the present day and not forward to the future. In every word and deed, we must live our lives today as if we were to die tonight. If we have a good conscience, we will not so greatly fear death. However, if we are not ready to die today, how will we be ready to die tomorrow? Tomorrow is not certain. We can't even guarantee there will be a tomorrow.

What does it profit us to live longer, but not live better? A long life doesn't become better, but often simply increases one's guilt. Oh, may we spend a single day in this world as we ought to spend it! Many people boast of how many years ago they invited Christ into their lives, but often there is very little evidence to show for it. It may be a fearful thing to die young, but perhaps it is more frightening to live long without God. Happy are people who are always thinking of the hour of their death and prepare daily to die. If you have ever seen a person die, keep in mind you will also pass away in the same way.

In the morning, reflect upon the fact that you may not see evening. And in the evening, don't boast about seeing the morning. We should always be prepared to die so that death will not find us unprepared. Many people die suddenly and unexpectedly. When the hour of death comes, we will soberly think of our lives. We must do so to avoid mourning bitterly that we have been so neglectful and lazy in fulfilling our God-given duties.

Happy and wise are people who now strive while living, for they will not have regrets in death. These things will give you confidence in a peaceful death: a godly contempt for worldly things, a fervent desire to live righteously, a love of discipline, the sorrow of true repentance, a willingness to obey, the denial of self, and submission to any adversity for the love of Christ. While we are in good health, we have many opportunities to do good works, but when we are ill we may not be able to do much. Few are made better by illness in the same way people who wander about the world seldom become holy.

So, we must not put off living out our salvation, for people will forget us sooner than we think. Now is the time to do good and help others. Now is the most important time. Now is the right time and the day of salvation. So, let us spend our time well now so we may lay up treasurers for ourselves in eternity. The hour will come when we will yearn for one more day—even one hour—to change our lives.

Dearly loved friends, we would free ourselves from great fears in this life if we would simply fear death! We should live now so at the hour of death we may rejoice rather than cower. We must learn to die to the world now, so we can begin to live with Christ now. Let us learn contempt for all earthly things now, so we may freely live with Christ. May we keep our bodies under control so we may live with sure confidence.

We must not be a fool and think we will live long when we can't be sure of one day! How many have been deceived and then suddenly have been snatched away from this body? How many times have we heard of one killed by violence, another drowned, another falling from a great height and breaking his or her neck, another dying at the table, or another at play? One died by fire, another by murder, another by a plague, another by a robbery. Death comes to all and life passes away like a shadow.

Who will remember us after our death? Work now, dearly beloved. Let us work all we can. We do not know when we will die. While we have time, let us lay up treasures in heaven for ourselves. Think of nothing except our own and others' salvation; care only for the things of God. "Then, when your earthly possessions are gone, they will welcome you to an eternal home" (Luke 16:9).

We must keep ourselves as strangers and pilgrims upon earth as if the things of this world don't apply to us. "For this world is not our permanent home; we are looking forward to a home yet to come" (Hebrews 13:14). May our daily prayers be filled with crying and tears so that our souls may be found worthy to pass happily after death unto our Lord. Amen.

Book 1 Chapter 23

89

ON THE FINAL DESIRE

*"Those who accept my commandments and obey them
are the ones who love me. And because they love me,
my Father will love them. And I will love them
and reveal myself to each of them."*

John 14:21

The Christ

My friends, if you want to be truly happy, I must be your
supreme and final desire. If I am your purpose, then your
love will be purified. Often people are sinfully focused on
themselves and created things. If you seek your own desires
in any matter, certainly you will become self-centered and
become spiritually barren. So, think of me first of all, for I
gave you all. Look upon each blessing as flowing from me
as their source.

From me, the humble and great, the poor and rich
draw water from me as a living fountain. Those who serve
me with a free and faithful spirit will receive grace on top

of grace. But people who take credit for any good or boast about the good in themselves will not receive true joy and love in their heart. They will be greatly hindered and be thrown into troubles. So, you must not take credit for any good and claim any virtue by your own effort, but credit it all to God, without whom you have nothing. I gave all. I will receive all again. I want you to give all thanks to me.

This is the truth, and by it all vain boasting is put to flight. If you receive my heavenly grace and true love, you will not be possessed by envy, hardness of heart, or self-love. For divine love conquers all things and increases the power of your soul. If you are truly wise, you will rejoice and hope in me alone. "Only God is truly good" (Luke 18:19). He is to be praised above all things and in all things to receive glory.

Book 3 Chapter 9

90

ON THE CLEAR DAY
OF ETERNITY

"Don't let your hearts be troubled.
Trust in God, and trust also in me.
There is more than enough room in my Father's home.
If this were not so, would I have told you
that I am going to prepare a place for you?
When everything is ready, I will come and get you,
so that you will always be with me where I am."

John 14:1-3

The Disciple

Oh, what blessed mansions we have in heaven! Oh, supreme Truth will ever enlighten us with the clear day of eternity, which the night cannot dim! The day is always joyful, always safe and secure, and never changing into anything contrary. Oh, I wish this day might shine forth now and that all temporal things would come to an end. God's glory shines on his children with unending brightness, but now from only afar and through dark glass since us, who are pilgrims on this earth.

The citizens of heaven know how glorious that day is. The exiled children of Eve groan, because this world is bitter and tiring. The days of this life are few and evil, full of sorrow and tough times. People are defiled with their sins, trapped with their passions, shackled with many fears, worn down with many cares, distracted with many questions, entangled with many trinkets, surrounded by many errors, worn down with many labors, weighed down with temptations, tempted by many pleasures, and tormented by poverty.

When will there be an end to all these evils? When will I be delivered from the wretched slavery of my sin? When will I concentrate on you, O Lord, alone? When will I rejoice fully in you? When will I truly be free from any hindrance, without any mental or physical burdens? When will I have solid, immovable, and secure peace—peace within and without, firmly on all sides? Blessed Savior, when will I stand and see you face to face? When will I gaze upon the glory of your kingdom? When will you be my all and all? Oh, when will I be with you in your kingdom, which you have prepared from the beginning of the world for those who love you? I am left impoverished, an exile in a hostile land where there are daily wars and terrible misfortunes.

Comfort my exile, relieve my sorrow for I long to be with you. Everything on earth is a burden to me as the world offers no comfort. I long to know you intimately, but I cannot here in this world. I long for heavenly things, but temporal things and sinful passions press upon me. In my mind, I want to be above all earthly things, but my human body brings me down. I am such a wretched person. I fight with myself. I am sadly disappointed with myself. My spirit seeks heavenly things, but my body desires things from below.

Oh how I inwardly suffer. While in my mind I meditate on heavenly things, earthly desires crowd in as I pray. My God, do not be far from me nor in anger desert your servant. "Hurl your lightning bolts and scatter your enemies! Shoot your arrows and confuse them!" (Psalm 144:6). Confuse the delusions of my enemy. Direct my senses to you, cause me to forget all worldly things. Help me to quickly cast away and despise all thoughts of sin. Nourish me, O Eternal Truth, that no mere human can influence me. Come to me, O Heavenly Delight, and let all impurity flee from your presence. Pardon me and gently treat me with your mercy whenever in prayer I think on anything besides you, for I confess I am continually distracted.

Often, when I am standing or sitting, I am somewhere else in my thoughts. Where my thoughts are, there I am. My thoughts are habitually drawn to your love which is delightful and pleasing.

So, you who are the Truth, has plainly said, "Wherever your treasure is, there the desires of your heart will also be" (Matthew 6:21). If I love heaven, I will gladly meditate on heavenly things. If I love the world, I will rejoice in the delights of the world and will be made sorry by its adversities. If I love physical things, then I will continually dwell on physical things. But if I love spiritual things, I will delight in meditating on spiritual things. For whatever things I love, I will talk about them and meditate on them in my home. Blessed are people who for your sake, O Lord, are willing to separate from all created things, who discipline their bodies and crucify sinful desires through the power of your Spirit. Then, with a peaceful conscience, they may offer up to you a pure prayer and be made worthy to rejoice with the heavenly choirs. They will have outwardly and inwardly shut themselves off from all worldly things.

Book 3 Chapter 48

ACKNOWLEDGMENTS

Thanks to my agent, Janet Kobobel Grant, and the wonderful people at Worthy Inspired for believing in this project and for the lightning speed in which the publishing house embraced the work and brought it to market. Pamela Clements and Bart Dawson are indeed "worthy" editors.

Thanks to my good friend and Catholic scholar, Michael Fraley, who patiently reviewed my work and vastly improved it by comparing my modernization with à Kempis's original Latin text. He has made sure this work accurately reflects the writing of our shared hero.

Most of all, thanks to my "Holy Ghost writer" for inspiring and energizing this project. *Soli Deo gloria!*

Other *Imitation of Christ* Resources

TheImitationOfChristDevotions.com

Other Books by James N. Watkins

Jesus: His Life and Lessons

Squeezing Good Out of Bad

Communicate to Change Lives

jameswatkins.com

ABOUT THE AUTHOR

James Watkins is the author of sixteen books including *Death & Beyond,* which won a Campus Life "Book of the Year" award, and *The Why Files* series, which was honored with a Christian Retailer's Choice award. He serves as associate acquisitions editor at Wesleyan Publishing House (Indianapolis) and has won four Evangelical Press Association awards for editing. James has also spoken in hundreds of churches, colleges, and conferences in the United States and around the world. He is a graduate of Indiana Wesleyan University with a BA in Theology and his graduate work is in communications at Ball State University and Purdue University. For fifteen years, James taught writing at Taylor University.

Thomas à Kempis has been a best-selling author for more than five hundred years. He was a priest, monk, and writer who lived in obscurity in fourteenth-century Germany. His words have changed lives for over five hundred years.

IF YOU ENJOYED THIS BOOK, WILL YOU CONSIDER SHARING THE MESSAGE WITH OTHERS?

Mention the book in a blog post or through Facebook, Twitter, Pinterest, or upload a picture through Instagram.

Recommend this book to those in your small group, book club, workplace, and classes.

Head over to facebook.com/worthypublishing, "LIKE" the page, and post a comment as to what you enjoyed the most.

Tweet "I recommend reading #TheImitationOfChrist by James N. Watkins // @worthypub"

Pick up a copy for someone you know who would be challenged and encouraged by this message.

Write a book review online.

WORTHY®
PUBLISHING

Visit us at worthypublishing.com

twitter.com/worthypub

worthypub.tumblr.com

facebook.com/worthypublishing

pinterest.com/worthypub

instagram.com/worthypub

youtube.com/worthypublishing